APR 1 3 200**DATE**

ill 4/2/07

DEC 0 8 2008

ill 7/13/16

Shadowland

Shadowland

William Arnold

McGraw-Hill Book Company

New York / St. Louis / San Francisco
Düsseldorf / Mexico / London / Toronto / Sydney

Book design by A Good Thing, Inc.
Copyright © 1978 by William Arnold.
All rights reserved.
Printed in the United States of America.
No part of this publication may
be reproduced, stored in a retrieval
system, or transmitted,
in any form or by any means,
electronic, mechanical, photocopying,
recording or otherwise, without the prior
written permission of the publisher.

234567890 DODO 78321098

Library of Congress Cataloging in Publication Data

Arnold, William, date
Shadowland
1. Farmer, Frances, 1914–1970.   2. Moving-picture
actors and actresses—United States—Biography.
Title
PN2287.F34A7   791.43′028′0924   [B]   78-4593
ISBN   0-07-002311-5

for kathie

Shadowland

Prologue

In the State of Washington, at a remote spot near the southern end of Puget Sound, there is a large complex of buildings known as the Western State Hospital at Steilacoom. It is situated on what is the oldest white settlement in the state and, during the Indian skirmishes of the 1850s, had actually been a frontier army post. Before the turn of the century the post was converted into a huge public insane asylum, but people still called it "Fort Steilacoom" and, shrouded as it usually is in the fog and mist that continually roll in from the Sound, its massive presence continues to evoke that name—fortresslike and forboding.

On a rainy fall day in 1948, the superintendent of this institution, a scholarly man named William Keller, arrived at his office. Observers recall that he invariably had a worried look on his face. He was, in fact, a very troubled man. Since the end of the war, the inmate population of his institution had almost doubled and he was totally unable to cope with the load. Thousands of patients were crowded into fourteen unattended wards and people who came to visit claimed that the place looked like a "Nazi concentration camp." A few months before,

9

Seattle newspapers reported the scandal: patients sleeping one against another on bare dirt floors; overcrowding so bad that the doctors had taken to indiscriminately administering shock treatments in order to keep the patients passive. Keller's staff doctors were threatening to resign if the conditions didn't improve, and there seemed no possibility of the legislature voting him any more funds in the foreseeable future.

While the overcrowding and horrific conditions had become intolerable, Keller believed he had at last found a solution. Earlier that morning he had welcomed America's most famous psychosurgeon to Steilacoom for what could be a historic event. This illustrious doctor had developed a "miracle" operation which would have a drastic effect on psychiatry and change the very nature of mental institutions forever. He claimed that he could stick an icepicklike instrument into a patient's brain and transform the most defiant maniac into a reasonable and obedient citizen. The doctor had come all the way to the wilds of Washington State to test this operation on the patients of Steilacoom, which just happened to include one very notable patient—in fact one of the most famous patients in the history of America's public mental hospitals—a former movie star named Frances Farmer.

This young woman had lived one of the strangest case histories on record. The doctors' diagnoses covered most of the classic symptoms in the clinical textbooks, but behind all of it was a woman with a lifelong impulse to rebellion, a powerful will to resist authority. Despite great accomplish-

10

ments in Hollywood and on Broadway, this unshakable will had put her in lifelong conflict with the powers that be and—after a number of bizarre episodes—she had finally ended up here. Because she was so famous and because she had offended so many powerful groups in her career, the institution was under enormous pressure to get results in her case—to demonstrate correction and rehabilitation. In the past four years, she had been given massive doses of insulin shock, electroshock, hydrotherapy, and experimental drugs. Yet nothing seemed to affect her. The most famous doctors in the world had stopped by to offer counsel, but not even they could suggest anything to break her incredible will.

Later that morning, Keller left his office and hurried to the operating theater in the next building. The room was already packed with visiting psychiatrists, hospital staff, and several photographers, and Keller stood in the rear and watched. The famous doctor was describing his procedure. He declared that he had helped develop the prefrontal lobotomy and that he felt it was now obsolete. His new operation, he claimed, could be administered as easily as a penicillin shot and would not even leave a scar. He said that its potential for controlling society's misfits—schizophrenics, homosexuals, radicals—was truly revolutionary and that he had already successfully performed the operation on a sane person.

As he concluded his briefing, the first woman was wheeled before him. He put electrodes to her temples and gave her electroshock until she passed out. Then he lifted her left eyelid and plunged the

11

icepick-shaped instrument under her eyeball and into her brain. Another woman was wheeled before him and he repeated the procedure, and then another woman and another and another, until Keller reputedly felt himself getting sick and had to leave the room.

An hour later, Keller returned to the operating theater and found everyone gone. He walked into the anteroom and looked at the postoperative patients resting on cots. One woman was silently weeping and several others were staring blankly at the ceiling. Near one end of the row of patients was Frances Farmer. She was, for all purposes, ready to be released. She would walk and talk and breathe exactly as before but there *was* a difference. From that moment on, she would no longer exhibit the restless, impatient mind and the erratic, creative impulses of a difficult and complex artist. She would no longer resist authority or provoke controversy. She would no longer be a threat to anyone.

1

I remember the first time I saw her. It was the summer of 1973, and I was twenty-seven years old and just starting a new job as editorial writer for the *Seattle Post-Intelligencer*. A suburban revival theater was running an old 1936 Goldwyn picture called *Come and Get It,* starring Edward Arnold, Joel McCrea, and someone named Frances Farmer. I had never even heard of Frances Farmer. When the lights went out and the scratchy old images flickered on the screen, I couldn't believe it. There is a scene in which Edward Arnold walks into a saloon and sees her for the first time and it is one of the great entrances of the movies, sheer magic. She was so incredibly beautiful, so hauntingly mysterious, so—I told the theater owner that I had never seen such an exciting star. And I never missed an old movie. Why had I never heard of this actress? What could possibly have become of her?

By the next morning, I still couldn't get Frances Farmer out of my mind. I had gone to the library and looked through dozens of dictionaries of film personalities and couldn't find a single entry under her name. Almost as an afterthought, I went to the card files at the newspaper to see if we might have something on her. Not only was there a Frances Farmer file but it was surprisingly thick. It was immediately apparent that (1) she had been born and raised in the city of Seattle (a startling coincidence) and (2) she had been an enormously controversial character. From a morning of reading through these cards, I was able to piece together this story: Frances Farmer had been one of the great stars of the late '30s and early '40s. Her rise in Hollywood and on Broadway had been called the greatest Cinderella story in the history of the American theater. At the age of twenty-one, she was considered the most promising young actress in the country, often compared with Garbo and Hepburn. She had been politically controversial—perhaps more so than any major star until Jane Fonda. At the very height of her fame, while still in her twenties, she had suddenly gone violently insane, was mysteriously committed to a public mental institution, and seemed to disappear forever.

When I began looking up old clippings and talking to old-time reporters around the city, I found there was even more to the mystery. It seemed that for the past thirty years, there had been vague rumors floating around the legal and journalistic circles of Seattle to the effect that there was a great untold story behind the Frances Farmer tragedy. Time and time again down through the years, people had stepped forward with strange stories about her—stories of the FBI and the CIA, of psychiatric abuse and medical atrocities and high governmental cover-up. Several writers in the '50s had investigated aspects of the case and had come up with

14

stories so bizarre that they could never be taken seriously. On top of this, a true-confession type of autobiography had been published two years after her death in 1970 and, though it was vague and seemed to be at least partially ghostwritten, it made certain unanswered charges that she had been subjected to inhumane treatment in the Washington State mental institution.

The fact that the beautiful and talented woman I had seen on film could go violently insane disturbed me profoundly. For days I couldn't get it out of my mind. At night I would dream about it. Finally, I went to my editor, a thirty-year veteran Seattle newspaperwoman named Ruth Howell, to talk about it. It turned out that she had actually known Frances Farmer slightly at the University of Washington and was almost as intrigued by the case as I was. She said something about it being an "upsetting" subject that "nobody wanted to talk about". I told her I wanted to dig up the records and track down the rumors and find out what really happened to Frances Farmer. My argument was fairly convincing. She had been a notable cultural figure. Her fate was essentially a mystery. Certain charges in connection with her commitment had been publicly made against the State of Washington and had gone unanswered. Mrs. Howell considered it carefully and gave me the go-ahead.

The next morning I sharpened three pencils and began an investigation, planning to spend at most a few weeks in the morgue and a few hours on the phone. As it turned out, I was to spend the next three years flying around the country, searching out

15

hundreds upon hundreds of fragmentary and often contradictory records—and from that investigation would emerge a story more bizarre than I could have imagined possible, a story that would touch the lives of some of the most prominent figures in Hollywood and New York and in the world of American politics and medicine. By the time I had fully comprehended the strange and terrible consequences of this story, I would never feel quite so secure or quite so confident about anything in my life again.

16

2

When people spoke of the story of Frances Farmer, they invariably managed to refer to it as a great "Hollywood" tragedy. A beautiful young Hollywood star at the peak of her career is inexplicably driven insane and vanishes into the snake pit of a public mental institution. Over and over again people who knew nothing about her would say she had been a fragile woman destroyed by Hollywood. An editor at *Variety* would tell me that hers was the greatest tragedy in the history of Hollywood ("far more tragic than, say, Marilyn Monroe or Judy Garland"). And yet every available record seemed to indicate that, except for a few brief years, the tragedy had little to do with Hollywood and was acted out almost entirely where it began—in the city of Seattle, Washington. Frances Farmer was born in Seattle. She became nationally controversial as a college student in Seattle. She constantly kept coming back to Seattle as a film star. Ultimately, she was involuntarily committed there.

Perhaps people were so quick to blame Hollywood because Seattle seems an unlikely place for such a tragedy to take place. Stuck off in the most rugged and remote corner of the United States,

17

it is a city of long expansive views and tall green trees, of blue skies in the summer, an invigorating light drizzle in the winter, and a stable and very healthy year-round temperature. It is America's youngest great city, settled by a predominantly Scandinavian influx as late as the 1880s and '90s. Its people still consider themselves first-generation pioneer stock. They are basically a proud and conservative people, and when I went around asking various civic boosters about Frances Farmer, a surprising number didn't want to talk about her. They would talk about Henry Jackson or Bing Crosby or Jimi Hendrix or even William O. Douglas. But the name Frances Farmer clearly struck a dissonant chord.

I had encountered this kind of reticence once before from the people of Washington State. Several years earlier, when I first moved there to go to college, I had tried to research the bloody labor battles that had torn the state apart in the teens and found it extremely difficult to find anyone who would talk about them. Seattle had been Northwest headquarters for the International Workers of the World—the infamous "Wobblies"—and the stomping grounds for Big Bill Haywood, Anna Louise Strong, Eugene V. Debs, and the like. Thousands of workers who had found the Northwest job market tightly controlled by the railroads and big lumber companies agitated not just for social reform but for a whole new political order to be born on the shores of Puget Sound and spread across the country. Radical labor had become so powerful by 1919 that it was able to engineer a general strike in Seattle—the first and only general strike that has ever taken place in America—an event which convinced most of the world that a Bolshevik Revolution was breaking out in the state but which, fifty years later, no one seemed willing to discuss on or off the record.

The local historians will tell you that this curious silence is largely due to a sense of "collective guilt" over some of the things that happened during those years, and perhaps there is some truth to this. The good people of Washington State were truly terrified by all this radical violence and they reacted to it violently, suppressing brutally the legions of idealistic Wobblies. In November, 1916, a group of Wobs who had been forcibly expelled from Seattle tried to land a ship several miles up the Sound at the town of Everett and went down in a hail of bullets, an event now celebrated in the history books as the Everett Massacre. In 1971, while trying to research a profile of Everett's own Senator Henry M. Jackson for the *Los Angeles Times,* I went around asking the old-timers of Everett about the Jackson family's connection to the massacre. It was impossible to find anyone who would admit even having heard of it. Similarly, just after World War I, the Wobblies' greatest hero, Wesley Everest, was hung and castrated by American Legionnaires just outside the town of Centralia, Washington. Today, you can walk into that sleepy little community and ask questions about that historic event and still get nothing but icy stares. The fact is that many of the people involved in those legendary vigilante actions are still alive and no one who is smart is talking about them.

19

But if the story of Frances Farmer was some-how tied to this old skeleton, there was certainly no hard evidence of it. I stopped trying to talk to people and spent a day in the Pioneer section of the Seattle Public Library, where I managed to find an entire file on her father, a Seattle attorney named Ernest Melvin Farmer. It seems that Mr. Farmer had been the son of a Minnesota State Supreme Court Justice who had advised all his children to go West. He came to Seattle to set up practice about the time the Klondike Gold Rush up in Alaska was building Seattle into the preeminent city of the Northwest. Although he appears to have been an amiable man without a great deal of ambition, his practice almost immediately prospered. He married a perky, re-cently divorced woman named Lillian Van Ornum, who ran the boarding house where he lived, and bought a home on Harvard Avenue in the fashion-able Capitol Hill district of town, where they soon had a son, Wesley, and a daughter, Edith. The file ends with World War I and the last entry states that on September 19, 1914 (at a time when they were both long past child-rearing age), the couple was unexpectedly blessed with a third child, an unusually vigorous and beautiful daughter named Frances.

The file also shows that on the morning of her birth, at almost the exact same moment, there had been a long and bloody battle between Seattle police and a group of Wobblies not far from her father's of-fice on the Seattle Skid Road—almost as if it were some kind of omen.

20

3

The details of Frances Farmer's first few years are still vague and shadowy. There are at least a dozen conflicting journalistic accounts floating around about those years, none of them particularly credible. *Life* magazine would say years later that she had lived in Hollywood and had even acted in films as a child, but, of course, this was probably only the whimsical notion of some long-forgotten press agent. The truth—as best I could discern it then—was that the Farmers moved back and forth between Washington, Oregon, and various places in California several times in those early years, but they had settled back in Seattle for good by the time Frances was eleven years old. She was raised in a big pink house still standing at 2636 47th SW in the residential suburb of West Seattle, a quiet, rather intelligent little girl, best remembered for her very large, almost extraordinarily beautiful blue eyes.

Most of these accounts agree that in the years between 1914 and 1920 the fortunes of the Farmer family declined rather drastically. E. M. Farmer was a kind but ineffectual man who seemed unwilling or unable to get in on the giant economic boom

21

Seattle was experiencing during and just after the World War. The labor situation upset him and nagged at his consciousness (to the absolute horror of his legal colleagues, he began to idolize the radical lawyer George Vanderveer, and had actually taken it upon himself to defend a number of indigent Wobs in court for free). On top of this he did not get along well with his wife—who he felt badgered him endlessly—and he eventually took to drink and sloth and, except for regular weekend visits, moved out of the house completely, an arrangement that would remain unchanged for the next twenty-five years.

When I left the Frances Farmer index and searched the newspaper morgue, I found more information on the early days of the Farmer family in Seattle. It seems that Lillian Farmer was a headstrong woman who by the early '20s had become something of a town character. For a period of years she was always on one campaign or another—against the bakeries of the city, which she tried to have closed down for selling nutritionally deficient products; against the Wobblies; against the school board (for teaching Communism); *for* patriotism (she made national news during World War I when she crossed a Rhode Island Red, a White Leghorn, and an Andalusian Blue to obtain a red, white, and blue chicken, which she called a "Bird Americana," and seriously lobbied to have replace the eagle as the national emblem). She was an exceptional (her nutritional hypotheses were years ahead of their time) if somewhat eccentric (she had once been arrested for shooting at her husband with a gun loaded with blanks) woman with an absolute genius for getting her name in the papers.

Using these accounts as a cross-reference, I was able, over a week or so, to line up a number of people still alive who had known the Farmers in those early days, and they all had essentially the same memories: poor old broken E. M. Farmer and his wildly outspoken wife, forever spouting her nutritional theories and patriotic sentiments, and the three well-behaved children, who always made the best marks in school. Everyone in West Seattle seemed to know the Farmers or know of them in those days. People would shake their heads and say that they were a family touched with brilliance and (as it later turned out) a certain madness. Indeed, it was difficult to determine where one left off and the other began.

I finally drove out to the old Farmer neighborhood in West Seattle, a pleasant fifteen-minute drive from the newspaper. It was a quiet middle-class section of small homes and well-kept lawns and tiny peekaboo views of Puget Sound here and there. (The actress Dyan Cannon, I am told, grew up in this same ideal middle-class American neighborhood.) I was able to pick out the old Farmer house almost at once. It was a large gabled house half hidden from the street by willow trees and a large fenced yard, a house with an unmistakably Gothic air of mystery and tragedy about it, now apparently unoccupied. It looked very much as if it might have been shunned by the rest of the neighborhood for the past thirty years.

The neighbors who remained from the old days—and there were a number of them—all remembered Frances Farmer. When I went around knocking on doors they couldn't understand why I would possibly be interested in that "sad old story" but they were quite willing to talk about it anyway. They told me they knew nothing about when she became a famous movie star and went crazy. They had read about it in the papers, of course ("Everyone did"), but that was all a big mystery to them. No, they had only known her in the early years when she was a young girl growing up around the neighborhood. Everyone in those days knew Frances Farmer.

She had—as far as anyone here knew—a relatively normal and happy childhood. She is remembered as a beautiful, inquisitive little girl who spent much of her time alone and showed signs of being slightly precocious. She attended the Lafayette Elementary School a few blocks away, where (the records still show) she was regarded as an exceptionally promising student who got along well with her classmates. She was something of a tomboy, forever tagging along after her older brother and sister or romping up and down SW 47th Street with her big German Shepherd or playing kick-the-can way into the evening twilight. Even now, after all that had happened to her, there are still people in that neighborhood to whom the mention of her name conjures up only the image of a scruffy little girl who would spend endless hours playing with her dog at the streetcar stop on California Avenue while waiting for her father to return home for his regular weekend visit.

Her tomboy period lasted longer than it did for most children, on into junior high, where she had little interest in dates and boyfriends, preferring to spend almost every weekend on hikes and camping trips with her family to the rugged Olympic and Cascade mountains that surround the city of Seattle. *Life* magazine later ran a full page of family pictures from this time. They show Frances preparing

25

for a family outing to the islands of Puget Sound, Frances on a camping trip with her father on Mount Rainier, Frances sitting on the running board of a Model T, mugging for the camera. One of the neighbors showed me a stack of family photographs from those days and they seem to picture the same ideal childhood and the same quiet, well-liked, and generally well-rounded girl her teachers would call a "credit to James Madison Junior High."

She entered West Seattle High School, a stately tan brick building just a few blocks down the street, in the fall of 1929. It was here that she came out of her pubescent shell and really began to blossom as a student. She got actively involved in school politics and displayed a genuine talent for debate and for writing poetry. After school, she began to spend long hours reading "serious" works of literature like *The Jungle* and *The Brothers Karamazov* and the essays of Nietzsche, all of which prompted her to form what her friends considered a number of very strong opinions very early in life. By the end of her first year at West Seattle High, she had become an extraordinarily pretty, mildly high-strung, fiercely outspoken young lady.

The people of West Seattle all seem to remember that Frances Farmer was an exceptional girl but they say she was "the kind of person who always did and said pretty much as she pleased." She was extremely considerate—kind and sensitive and generous almost to a fault, especially to animals and anyone she considered underprivileged—except in one curious way. She seemed incapable of dissembling—those polite evasions and omissions that ease social intercourse. In fact, she could not abide anything or anyone she openly knew to be dishonest. She would not fib to protect a classmate. If someone asked her opinion they would get it, no matter how unpleasant or abrasive. If she believed in something strongly enough, there was no way she could be shaken from that conviction. It was perhaps her most prominent trait, this tenacious and often rather brutal honesty, and it would get her in trouble all her life, beginning publicly when she was sixteen years old.

There is a great number of existing versions of this first great controversy which did so much to shape the rest of Frances Farmer's life. The press of the time was full of accounts of how a young girl had shocked and scandalized the city of Seattle. There is an even more detailed (and, as it turned out, considerably more accurate) version of it in a 1936 *Collier's* magazine. And there are still other (significantly watered-down) versions of it in the glut of true-confession material and the book that appeared under her name after her death. But when I left the public library and called the West Seattle High Alumni Association, I discovered there were actually people still alive who were directly involved and who could, if anyone cared, tell the true story of that extraordinary episode.

It began innocently enough in April, 1931, when Frances was a junior in high school. She had entered a creative writing class taught by Miss Belle McKenzie, a controversial (she was rumored to have radical leanings), fiery, redhaired woman who seemed to be everybody's favorite teacher at West Seattle in those days. She was the first person to recognize the remarkable penchant for candor in

28

Frances, to appreciate the young girl's highly developed sense of irony, and to encourage it, and she became the most important single influence on Frances' life. It took me nearly a week of steady searching to find Belle McKenzie. She was a white-haired lady in her eighties, living out a quiet retirement on Washington's remote Kitsap Peninsula. She was still clearheaded, still outspoken, and still "haunted by the memory of Frances Farmer."

She remembered the affair with the immediacy of a recent event. The class was having a writing competition and Frances had worked on and polished an essay on a subject that seemed particularly compelling to her. The subject was the death of God. The essay was called "God Dies," and it was by any measure an astute, ironic, beautifully executed piece of writing. She told how she had misplaced her new hat one day and had prayed to God to help her find it—which He apparently did. Later she learned that a classmate's parents had been killed in an accident and she was outraged at the injustice of a God who would answer her trivial prayer and still permit such a tragedy. From a worn and yellowing piece of notebook paper I read the fading typewritten words:

> ... God became a super father who wouldn't spank me. But if I wanted a thing badly enough, He arranged it.
>
> That satisfied me until I began to figure out that if God loved all His children equally, why did he bother about my hat and let other children lose their fathers and mothers for al-

29

ways? I began to see that He didn't have much to do about people's dying or hats or anything. They happened whether He wanted them to or not, and He stayed in heaven and pretended not to notice. I wondered a little why God was such a useless thing. It seemed a waste of time to have Him. After that, He became less and less, until He was nothingness.

I felt rather proud to think that I had found the truth by myself, without help from anyone. It puzzled me that other people had not found [sic] too. God was gone.

Belle McKenzie was so impressed she entered the essay in the *National Scholastic* magazine's student writing competition, then the most prestigious student contest in the country. It won first prize. Frances got $100 and created a furor.

It seemed that in 1931 the city of Seattle was not ready for such theories about the death of God, particularly from its schoolchildren. News coverage of the award-winning essay snowballed from a short item in the *Post-Intelligencer* around the first of the month (LOCAL GIRL WINS WRITING AWARD) to page-one features in the *Star* and *Times* (SEATTLE GIRL DENIES GOD AND WINS PRIZE), and was eventually picked up by the major wire services. By the second week, letters were pouring into the Farmer home from outraged Christians up and down the West Coast and across the country, charging Frances with being a dupe of "Godless Communism." (As one of the city's leading anti-Communists, Frances' mother Lillian must have been particularly upset by these charges, but she strongly defended her daughter's essay in several interviews.) By the end of the month, it had gotten to the point where churches all over the city were actually holding emergency sessions to discuss the "rampant atheism" in the public school system. The name of Frances Farmer was being denounced from a hundred pulpits as the foremost example of pagan youth. ("If the young people of this city are going to hell," one Baptist minister told his congregation, "Frances Farmer is surely leading them there.")

Belle McKenzie still looked incredulous when she spoke about it all those years later. "It was so stupid," she said. "It was all over *nothing*. Nothing at all." And yet it was the beginning of Frances' national reputation as a troublemaker. People began to call her the "Bad Girl of West Seattle" and avoid her completely, and all the publicity very nearly kept her from being accepted to college. It was all a shocking experience for a withdrawn sixteen-year-old, and it only served to make her more withdrawn, more high-strung, more rebellious.

The year following the commotion over the "God Dies" essay, Frances Farmer seemed to stay very much within herself. The experience had no doubt left her deeply scarred, but it also must have given her confidence in her literary ability, because she continued turning out short stories and poetry all that year. She also decided during that year that she would enter the University of Washington after graduation and major in journalism. Both her brother Wesley and sister Edith were already in the School of Journalism there, and it seemed like the "logical thing to do." She told Belle McKenzie that she planned to earn her living as a reporter or a lawyer but her real goal in life was to develop into a "successful poet."

In the middle of this last year before college, another traumatic event took place in Frances' life—her parents officially divorced. Though he had not lived at home for years, E. M. Farmer had always resisted this idea and often spoken of his hopes for a reconciliation. For some unknown reason, Lillian suddenly got herself a lawyer in early 1932 and won a fast divorce, and for the rest of her life she would be in a constant legal battle with him over support. There is little doubt that, more than the other children, Frances loved and identified with —and certainly physically resembled—her father. The divorce made no material difference to her life but it had a considerable psychological impact on her, and many of her friends would later say she was never quite able to forgive her mother for it.

Because her mother seemed such an integral part of the mystery of Frances Farmer, I spent some time trying to find out more about Lillian. I spoke to her lifelong attorney and numerous friends and neighbors, and they all described her as an "impressive" woman. Well over six feet in height, with large bones and a hawklike face, she was a commanding personality with an opinion about everything. Born Lillian Van Ornum, the daughter of "freethinking" pioneers in Roseburg, Oregon Territory, in 1874, she had come to Seattle via a circuitous route that had taken her all over California (she was largely raised in Chico), Alaska, and Idaho. Previously married and divorced in San Francisco, she already had a daughter named Rita when she married E. M. Farmer in 1905. Underneath the newspaper headline eccentricities, the people who knew her say she was a "fine woman," one who constantly took in foster children and stray animals, and who always was the first to lend a hand in a crisis—a woman, as one informant pointed out, not unlike "the mother on *The Waltons*." Her attorney, the truly distinguished Seattle feminist Lady Willie Forbus, told me Mrs. Farmer was one of the finest women she ever met, a great champion of the women's movement and of the cause of nutrition.

33

During the month I was talking to the friends of Lillian Farmer, the autobiography of Frances Farmer, called *Will There Really Be a Morning?*, hit the paperback stands. I spent an entire day and night reading and studying this book that told how Frances had gone insane under the pressures of family and stardom and been callously incarcerated in an unnamed mental institution. The book moved me to tears and rage and yet there were things about it that bothered me. From a quick comparison with the newspaper files, I could tell that much of it was simply inaccurate, that many of the names used were fictitious, and whole incidents and scenes had obviously been fabricated. Over and over again, the voice of Frances says "I don't remember" and speaks of "great gaps in her recall" and "periods of blackout." I called the editor of the book in New York. He told me that Frances was in "sad shape" toward the end and did have tremendous problems recalling whole years of her life. He said that in fact a friend of Frances in Indianapolis had done most of the actual writing of the book.

But whatever the authenticity of the book—and there will be more on that later—somewhere in it there is the unmistakable voice of Frances Farmer, and that voice wholeheartedly names her mother as the source of a life of problems. It portrays Lillian Farmer as an ogre out of *Grimm's Fairy Tales,* an absolute monster of a mother who singlehandedly destroys her daughter and enjoys it in the process. "Who," she writes, "was responsible for the pain? Certainly I contributed to my agonies, but there was another villain. . . . There is a Jewish saying, 'God could not be everywhere and therefore He made mothers,' and whether I was justified or not, I held mine accountable as the main root of my despair." Many other people, including Belle McKenzie and friends of Frances in later life, would confirm this vision and describe Lillian as an altogether "horrible" person.

Many times during the next few years I would run into this seeming paradox regarding Lillian V. Farmer. She was always described either as a hardworking, self-sacrificing woman who did nothing but good works or as a publicity-seeking, domineering shrew who destroyed her family. Her image changed like a chameleon; she seemed a mass of contradictions; yet Lillian Farmer had room enough in her psyche to be both of these people. She was highly intelligent and extremely eccentric. She was a strong-willed, uncompromising woman who did many irrational things because she had a strong-willed, uncompromising daughter. She was the kind of woman for whom being a mother was everything, and yet she would do things in the name of motherhood that would seem almost unthinkable.

7

I drove out to the University of Washington. The school occupies a large wooded area across town from West Seattle on a bluff overlooking Lake Washington. It is one of the largest and most visually splendid campuses in America, a veritable storybook setting of towering evergreens, expansive grassy landscapes, and tall Gothic buildings. On a plaque in the administration building there was a list of its most famous alumni. There were names of politicians and admirals and obscure artists. There was, however, no mention of the name of Frances Farmer. Despite the fact that she was easily the most successful actress the university ever produced, there was not a single mention of her in the back issues of the alumni magazine. No Frances Farmer memorial fountain. Nor even had the students of the drama department ever heard of her.

But when I spoke to some of the drama staff who had been there in the early '30s, it was a different story. They all remembered Frances Farmer. She had been an enormously beautiful and talented and well-liked student there. She had also been a determined radical who had triggered one of the greatest controversies the university had ever experienced. ("Later, you know, she went mad.") Why, they said, there had never been a story quite like it and there had to be reams of records somewhere. I listened to their stories and then went up to the university library Northwest bibliography section where, sure enough, there was a manila file stuffed with neatly mounted clippings which made her strange career as a student very easy to trace.

It was the depth of the Depression when Frances arrived at the university, and with no financial help from home, she had to work her way through college in all the traditional ways for a young Seattle girl—as waitress at the Mount Rainier Lodge, salesgirl at the Bon Marché Department store, typist, usherette at the downtown Paramount Theater (where, ironically, she later claimed she developed a lifelong contempt for the movies, which she considered a "dishonest" art). She commuted to campus from home, avoided the fraternity and sorority crowd, and apparently had no boyfriends that anyone can remember. In that first difficult year she worked twenty-hour days, read everything she could get her hands on, and spent what little free time came her way alone in her room working and reworking her poetry.

Her literary ambitions were not well received at the University of Washington. Women were not taken very seriously in the Journalism School in those days, particularly women as beautiful as Frances Farmer, and whenever she tried to do something original, it was generally met with rejection. She published one poem in the University of Wash-

37

ington *Daily* which was supposed to have shown promise (after days of searching I was unable to find it), but no one encouraged her to do more. When she joined the *Daily* staff, as was required of all journalism majors, she was given the thoroughly undesirable task of covering the campus infirmary. She quickly tired of writing about sore throats, and she found she didn't get along with the staid, conservative students who staffed the *Daily*. At the end of her freshman year, she quit the paper in frustration and gradually drifted away from journalism entirely.

At the beginning of her sophomore year, she managed to fall in with a scruffy, "artistic" crowd that centered around the university art and drama departments. These students spoke boldly about such things as artistic integrity and the inevitability of socialism, and Frances found them and everything they said irresistibly attractive. She became something of a hanger-on to this crowd, which was led by a radical young drama instructor named Sophie Rosenstein, included such future notables as Jane Rose, Tom Powers and a husky, notoriously reckless boy named Chet Huntley, a star of university plays who later became a famous newscaster. Several of these people would later say that Huntley fell in love with Frances and that they had embarked upon a brief but serious romance. I called Huntley at his luxurious Montana resort to ask him about this and after an agonizing pause he muttered something about "the most beautiful girl he had ever known" and "tragic story" and then hung up.

Whatever their relationship had been, Huntley was at least partially responsible for introducing her to the world of the theater. He took her along to his rehearsals and suggested she try out for a walk-on. It was very strange. Though she had no previous exposure, she seemed to know at once that she had found her calling. She fell instantly in love, hopelessly stagestruck, enchanted by the very idea of the Stanislavsky "method" of acting that was just then becoming the rage. The theater was, like writing, a means of expressing herself, but a purer, more direct, more (her favorite word) "honest" form of artistic expression. She wanted entree to that world in the most passionate way and she utterly dedicated herself to the task. She went so far as to tell her new friends that she would not be satisfied until she had become a member of what was then the purest, most famous element of the American drama—New York's Group Theater.

By this time a tall, beautiful young woman with a broad forehead and high delicate cheekbones, she changed her major, began appearing in small roles in university productions, and was almost immediately successful. She made a striking stage presence—with a stunning profile and a deep distinctive voice that would become a trademark—and there was a mysterious aura about her that made audiences stand up and take notice the minute she stepped on a stage. Professor Glenn Hughes, head of the drama department, recognized that quality at once ("Whatever it is that makes a star," he would tell his classes for years afterward, "she had it, and you knew it the minute you looked at her"). He soon had her playing the leads in *Uncle Vanya* and *Helen of Troy,* in which she displayed surprising depth and exciting potential.

In the fall of 1935, she played the part of Elsa Brandt in Sidney Howard's *Alien Corn,* a difficult leading role for which she worked day and night for some five weeks to prepare herself. Her interpretation of the young musician who is stifled by a provincial environment was so startling that she created something of a citywide sensation. The downtown newspaper critics left the theater saying they had frankly never seen such a performance in a nonprofessional production. (One critic wrote: "Frances Farmer has that mysterious something that separates the actress from the hack. . . . She has a divine intangible maturity to her acting that is destined for the lights of Broadway.") The fact that this was the same girl who had scandalized the city a few years earlier with an essay on the death of God, made her success doubly newsworthy. It seemed that without even trying she had once again become a public figure.

8

But Frances' moment of glory at the University of Washington did not last and was soon soured by yet another controversy—this one far more serious than the essay scandal and far more political in nature. It began with a strange series of events in her junior year and mushroomed far out of proportion until it made her name almost synonymous with Northwest Communism in the mid-'30s. Although it is (incredibly) barely mentioned in most of the meager source material on her life, this controversy became one of the biggest news stories of the time (in the newspaper file under "Communism—Washington State" it is, in fact, the largest entry) and easily the single most formative event of her entire life.

In early 1935, the state's long-standing problem with radical labor suddenly erupted into another major crisis. The same left-wing political factions which were so brutally beaten down in the teens had been given a giant shot in the arm by the Depression. (Radical labor had gotten so powerful that several members of Roosevelt's Cabinet had taken to referring publicly to the "forty-seven states and the Soviet of Washington.") This situation had

41

been building all through the early '30s, and by the end of 1934, the downtown business interests decided that they had had enough. Suddenly it was the violent days of the Wobblies and the Everett Massacre all over again. In January, 1935, a group of some four thousand prominent Seattle citizens calling themselves "The American Vigilantes of Washington" dramatically came forward with the results of a two-year secret investigation which "proved" there was an enormous Communist conspiracy in the Northwest ("insidiously creeping into unions, churches, schools, and universities") bent on no less than a major revolution. The vigilantes then proceeded to counter this revolution by raiding bookstores, burning books, busting heads, and generally goading the FBI and Seattle police into arresting anyone even vaguely suspected of Communist agitation.

This vigilante action had a devastating effect on the students of the drama department. Nowhere was sympathy with radicalism more pronounced than on the university campus, and nowhere on campus was it more deeply rooted than in the drama department. Frances' political concern had been steadily growing ever since she changed her major—many of her closest friends had been involved in demonstrations and what the newspapers were calling "Red Riots" on the streets of Seattle, and she had been shocked at the casually brutal way freedom of speech was being clubbed down by Seattle police. As a leader of the drama students, she felt compelled to speak out on this and other great issues of the day at the student forum and various drama assemblies. She also began to hand out leaflets, pass around petitions, and even to attend a few radical meetings and pro-Communist rallies at the UW commons (much as thousands of others would do thirty years later at the exact same spot over another great issue).

At the very height of this crisis, Seattle's Communist newspaper, *The Voice of Action*, decided to sponsor a subscription drive contest at the university which would focus attention on student support for the radical labor movement. The newspaper was essentially a small operation run by a handful of university dropouts whose main function and great delight was to provoke the business establishment, to which end they would go to almost any length. (The county prosecutor, a rising young lawyer named Warren G. Magnuson, had arrested the editors of the paper for "criminal libel" and it was a favorite target of the vigilantes.) The purpose of the contest was to get publicity, and the name which would obviously give them the most publicity was that of Frances Farmer, the sympathetic star of the drama department. Two radical students went to her through her mentor, Sophie Rosenstein, and asked for permission to sell subscriptions in her name, which she enthusiastically granted them. On March 10, 1935, it was announced that she had won the contest. The first prize was a VIP tour of the Soviet Union.

When this news got out, once again a tremendous outcry arose in the city over Frances Farmer. At no time in the long and turbulent history of radicalism in the Northwest has a single incident stirred such an uproar. A pretty young Seattle girl, the pride of the university drama department, was going to Russia under the auspices of the Communist Party! Nothing could have more dramatically symbolized to the average Seattle middle-class family the act of their children being taken away from them by World Communism. The vigilantes vowed they would never let it happen. Fighting broke out between the *Voice of Action* people and a group of vigilantes at the Seattle YMCA, where a banquet that had been scheduled to honor Frances had been canceled because of city pressure. The newspapers had a field day, aided by Frances' mother, who on hearing the news became firmly convinced that her daughter had become a Communist and held daily press conferences to express her indignation. ("The Soviet dagger has struck deep in the heart of America," she told the *Seattle Post-Intelligencer*.)

The story appeared on the front pages of the Seattle papers and was almost immediately picked up by the national wire services. After a few days, Frances became frightened by the bitter tone of the publicity and went down to the Seattle *Times* newsroom and typed out a disclaimer statement that appeared on page one under the head WHY I AM GOING TO RUSSIA. She wrote:

> No country is more interesting than Russia at this time, both artistically and scientifically. My interest in it, and my delight at the opportunity to go there and see things at first hand, is purely artistic. I am interested in the Russian Drama.

44

I am not interested in the country scientifically. Certainly I am not interested in it politically. Naturally I'm interested in all forms of government. Communism has no more appeal for me than any other form of government. I am not a Communist.

I don't know anyone who wouldn't give a great deal to be able to make the trip offered me, no matter in what particular field his interest lies.

I happen to be absorbed in the theater. Russia is artistically one of the most interesting and outstanding in the world. The chance to view at first hand one of the ten most important theatrical centers is the best thing that could happen to me.

Naturally anyone aware of the European situation politically could have no better opportunity to make an unbiased judgment than the one a personal survey offers. I look upon my trip as a purely educational pursuit. I have no doubt that I will gain an understanding that I have not had before.

The disclaimer had little effect. The day after her explanation appeared, she picked up a newspaper with a banner headline proclaming CO-ED STILL DETERMINED TO ACT FOR REDS.

9

For days, the controversy over Frances Farmer raged in the newspapers of Seattle and cities across the country. Some of the headlines that appeared that March give an indication of the heart of the controversy that ensued: MOTHER WARNS AGAINST RED TEACHERS; MOTHER UN- COVERS RED VICE RING; SEATTLE GIRL AIDS REDS. Frances moved to an apartment in the university district to get away from the tension at home, and teams of reporters drove back and forth daily, play- ing the story, building the suspense. Would she go or wouldn't she?

The public dispute between mother and daughter had sparked so much publicity that Lillian Farmer held a press conference at the end of the week to clarify her position. "I am afraid the Com- munists will influence my daughter against her coun- try—without her realizing what they are doing . . . ," she told the reporters assembled at her home. "I cannot bear to see her go under the wing of the Communist agencies. She does not know the Rus- sian language. I am afraid that innocently and without recognizing the subversive principles be- hind the thing, Frances will be presented to her Russian audiences as a Communist representative from American universities. They may even use her to solicit funds to be used to spread Communist propaganda in the United States—to cut the throat of her own country."

Over the next few weeks, Lillian Farmer became, really, an advocate for all those parents who felt threatened by the radicalism of their children, a role which she seemed to enjoy immensely. Her quotations ("If I must sacrifice my daughter to Communism, I hope other mothers save their daughters before they are turned into radicals in our schools") were printed in bold 18-point italics under banner headlines. Under the kicker A SEATTLE MOTHER'S WARNING she lambasted the University of Washington and Frances' teacher Sophie Rosenstein (whom she held personally responsible for Frances' downfall): "The University and high schools are hotbeds of Communism. In the contest, Frances and those supporting her had a list of University and high school teachers who were interested in the labor movement. They helped her get subscriptions to the paper. . . . Something should be done immediately to clean the schools of radical teachers before they sway other girls and boys away from American ideas. . . ." She spoke of how their children were being slowly poisoned by Red propaganda. "It is all done so subtly," she said. "I've heard results of it in the conversations of the young people. They say that the talk about suffering in Russia is all propaganda. They sneer at American traditions. They say who was George Washington, anyway, but a rebel, and Grant a drunkard and that this is a nation of hero worshipers. . . .They quote their teachers that the Constitution is outmoded and government a farce, and they talk about Russia's five-year plan. Some of these teachers have encouraged these boys and girls to go to Communist meetings. When are the parents going to wake up?!''

It must have been the most agonizing decision Frances had ever had to make in her young life. She had never disputed her mother before—about anything—but this was different. The trip was her once-in-a-lifetime chance to get out of Seattle and see the world and she was not about to lose it because of what people might think. ("That would be cheap and dishonest," she argued.) She talked it over with her father and Belle McKenzie, both of whom agreed with her, and on the morning of March 30, 1935, she packed her bags and went down to the Seattle Central Bus Station with a group of friends for the first leg of the long trip east.

Lillian Farmer came down to see her off. She stood resolutely in front of the bus and made one last effort to stop her. "You're breaking my heart, Frances," she said.

Frances put her arms around her and whispered in her ear, "I'll be all right—don't worry, Mother." Then she kissed her and climbed into the bus.

Before the bus was out of sight, Mrs. Farmer stepped before the flock of reporters and read the following statement: "There has been no break between Frances and me over the trip. My fight has been with the publication for sending her to Russia where she will be thrown in full contact with people

48

who probably will make every effort to persuade her to Communism." That said, she turned and went home.

The cross-county trip was chronicled by the national wire services like a major sporting event. When the bus pulled into Spokane on its first stop, a large and curious crowd had gathered to gawk at the girl Communist from Seattle, and she was whisked to a reception and luncheon at the Spokane Communist Party Headquarters. For hours, speakers told of the wonders of Moscow, the new order about which they could only dream, but which this young girl would soon "actually witness in person." Afterward, a press conference was set up during which, according to press accounts, Frances appeared nervous, frightened, and anxious to get the whole thing over with.

Q. How long have you been a Communist, Frances?

A. I am not a Communist.

Q. Then what is your purpose for making this trip?

A. I believe . . . I think this trip will be a marvelous chance to see Russia and study the Soviet Union.

Q. Can you tell us what you intend to bring back from this great journey?

A. I intend to bring back an unbiased report of my observations.

That night she left for Chicago, where she got

49

a similar reception ("I am not a Communist," she had to keep insisting to everyone she met), and arrived in New York the first part of April, where she was greeted with comparatively little fanfare. She was escorted around the city by a delegation of local Communist leaders and—through an introduction written by Sophie Rosenstein—got herself invited to a party given by members of her cherished left-wing Group Theater (at which she first met a soaring young playwright named Clifford Odets). On April 10, she booked third-class passage on the *Manhattan* and sailed for Europe.

10

The journey to Russia in 1935 was the most dramatic event in the early life of Frances Farmer, and I wanted to know as much about it as possible. Two researchers joined me and we spent the better part of a month digging through press accounts, writing Soviet officials (who were no help at all), and looking up people she might have spoken to before or after the trip. The most curious thing that turned up was the fact that the scholars we interviewed for background all seemed to be familiar with the story of how the American coed had defied the city of Seattle and toured Russia for the Communists. It was one of the most sensational stories in the context of American-Soviet relations in the '30s and it seems extraordinary that in later years powerful movie moguls would be able to keep it virtually secret from most of the moviegoing public. In any case, what actually happened on that trip is still shrouded in mystery (the trip itself is barely even mentioned in the autobiography). There are only a few yellowing letters and the accounts she gave the press and a few close friends, and they don't really present a very clear picture of her thoughts.

She had every reason to be terrified when

51

she stepped on the deck of the *Manhattan* that spring morning. She had just turned twenty years old. She had never left home before. She was embarking on a long, rugged journey to a country the newspapers were daily proclaiming a "living hell," and being escorted by people her parents had told her were the sworn enemies of her own country. Most terrifying of all was the fact that she was doing it all entirely alone. And yet there is no indication that she displayed the slightest hesitation about going. As usual, she seemed all gritty determination and strength of purpose and she clearly regarded this rather perilous odyssey as nothing less than a grand adventure.

The crossing on the crowded, stuffy ship took weeks. From Southampton, she boarded a Soviet ship to Bremerhaven and then took a train across a Depression-ravaged Eastern Europe (stopping briefly in Berlin, Warsaw, and Leningrad), during which she witnessed, for the first time in her life, unparalleled poverty and human suffering. When she got to Moscow, she was greeted by a group of Party officials and immediately taken on a lengthy tour of the showcase factories and collective farms. Over the next few days, she stood in the reviewing stand for the May Day demonstration, attended a ballet and an army concert at the Bolshoi Theater, and met leaders of the Politburo, all of whom assumed she was the representative of America's Communist youth, just as her mother had warned they would.

Moscow of the mid-'30s was, in its own way, one of the most exciting cities on earth. Artists and engineers and political idealists from all over Europe had flocked there to take part in a great experiment in socialism. As she gradually adjusted to the cultural shock, Frances became genuinely impressed with the energy of the place and the dedication of the people she met. She told her Russian hosts of the labor problems of the Northwest, of her and her classmates' ideas about socialism and their hopes for the future of America. She also argued with them about the things she couldn't accept. On May Day she managed to offend Party leaders assembled to meet her by commenting on the poverty she saw everywhere and by defending her country when a cheap swipe was taken ("I am an American, after all," she supposedly told one of them). Her unswerving candor on every subject was more than a little disconcerting to them. She was clearly not what they had in mind for the representative example of America's Communist youth.

Still, the trip seemed to have a profound effect on her thinking. Most everything she had been told about Russia—from both sides of the political spectrum—had been false, or at the very least biased. The Russian people were trying to order their country after centuries of exploitation in the only way that seemed to work for them, and she respected them for it. Most of all, the trip showed her that she could accomplish something on her own. The whole experience was a kind of test for her, she later said, which she had passed, and it strengthened her personal determination to make something of her life and further widened the gap between herself and the rest of her family. "I have seen the world," she wrote home,"and now I am ready to make my mark on it."

She returned to New York aboard the *President Cleveland* at the end of May, 1935. As the ship was docking, bands of reporters flocked to hear her "unbiased report" on the Soviet Union. Standing there on the pier, she told them that Russia was even more fascinating than her wildest expectations. She had witnessed a "most spectacular" May Day parade and ridden in the new Moscow subway and thought it "a marvelous piece of work." Finally she said, "I have never been definitely a Communist. My whole interest is in the theater. I'm an actress, or trying to be. But I came back more excited than ever about Russia, which is a marvelous place for any art. My sympathy and support are all for Russia."

That statement appeared under banner headlines in newspapers in Seattle and other cities across the country—a calculated slap in the face to the American Vigilantes of Washington and everyone else who had tried so desperately to keep her from going. In later years, like so many of the things she would say and do, it would come back to haunt her.

11

To pick up Frances' trail again after the Russian adventure, I flew to New York City for a few days before going on to Hollywood. Using old press accounts and a Manhattan phone book, I found her first agent and several people who claimed to have known her well in the weeks after the landing of the *President Cleveland*. These people all readily acknowledged they knew nothing at all about her later insanity but they did know quite a bit about how she became a star. Like everything else in her life, it happened suddenly and not without a good deal of controversy. These people were "amazed" that it was not better known because for sheer fairy tale drama and triumph of will it was a story almost unequaled in the annals of Hollywood.

It seems that after the publicity died down, Frances decided to forget college and stay on in New York to fulfill her dreams of becoming a great actress. She wrote her father and told him she felt she had to stay as far away from Seattle as possible to escape the radical image that had brought so much shame on her family. She moved into a Greenwich Village apartment with a friend from

Seattle named Jane Rose, who was doing graduate drama work at Columbia (and who, incidently, would become famous thirty years later as the dotty mother-in-law on the television series *Phyllis*), and together they began making the rounds of the Broadway casting offices. Frances took a few small modeling jobs from an ad agency to pay her share of the rent and generally settled in for what she thought would be a long hard struggle for success.

The struggle did not turn out to be either long or particularly hard for her. Within two weeks of landing, she came under the influence of an enthusiastic small-time agent named Shepard Traube, who immediately recognized her potential. There are two different versions of how this came about, a dispute which would later figure prominently in a lawsuit between them. The first was that Frances had met a young doctor on the return ship from Europe who had fixed her up with an introduction to Traube. The second, and more likely, version is that Traube, an ambitious young man who operated out of a small office on 42nd Street, spotted Frances' picture in the *New York Times* just before her Russian adventure and sought her out on his own initiative. In either case, it was apparent that he took one look at her and decided she was star material. ("I'll take you on," he said, "but you'll have to work your behind off for me.") He signed her to a seven-year personal contract and took her to see Oscar Serlin, who was then New York talent chief for Paramount Pictures.

Serlin—a large, blustery man who later

became the producer of *Life with Father* and other Broadway hits—looked her over noncommittally and set up a screen test. He then drove her out to the Paramount studios on Long Island himself. At the studios, makeup man Eddie Senz cut her hair into a bob, shaved her eyebrows, plastered a layer of makeup on her face, and put her in front of a camera to act out a scene from *The Lake* with another newcomer named Allyn Joslyn. When the test was developed, it confirmed everything Traube and Serlin suspected. On film she exuded a Garbo-like beauty and intelligence—"You just couldn't keep your eyes off her," Serlin would later say. He was particularly struck by her voice, a very precise, resonant voice with a haunting quality that lingered in the mind long after the image had faded. After approval came back from the West Coast some weeks later, he offered her a contract. "I think you have the potential to be a very big star," he told her.

The whole thing was like some incredible schoolgirl fantasy. Within a few weeks of getting back to the country—without even trying, really—she had been offered a substantial contract with a major Hollywood studio. She was very flattered and very excited. But she was also doubtful and she frankly told them so. It was a dream come true all right, but it was not *her* dream. Her goal was the legitimate theater. Hollywood was against all the "artistic" principles she had acquired at the university and everything she had believed all her life.

The one thing that all the people involved seem to remember is that Frances Farmer left New York primed for a fight she could not possibly win.

She needed the financial security and the ego gratification the contract offered. So she would play the game for a while, but she was not about to compromise her larger goals. The prospect of movie stardom was an intriguing new challenge for her, but she intended to pursue it on her own terms and only as a temporary detour on her way to Broadway. When Serlin placed the contract before her, she signed it, packed her bags, and—determined as ever—set out to do battle with the Philistines of Hollywood.

12

The day Frances Farmer arrived in Hollywood—October 5, 1935—Clark Gable was
filming *San Francisco* on the Metro lot and Bette
Davis had just won her first Oscar. The biggest hits
in town were *Top Hat, Captain Blood,* and *Lives of
a Bengal Lancer.* The motion-picture industry,
which had just enjoyed one of the most profitable
years in its history, was at the very height of its
power and influence over American life. A matter of
weeks before, Frances had been in Moscow as a
guest of the Communist Party, watching the Sovi-
ets trying to create a new world order based on pu-
ritanical equality, and now, suddenly, she found
herself a functioning part of what those same people considered the mecca of decadent capitalism.
She was assigned to Paramount's charm school
with a dozen or so other new contract players, all
of whom were grubbing for recognition like so
many characters out of *The Day of the Locust.* As
forceful as she was talented, Frances was put directly to work.

When I first got to Hollywood in May, 1974,
I immediately drove out to the Paramount lot in a
rundown residential area just off Melrose Avenue. I

59

tried to find someone who could tell me about Frances' early days at the studio. I spoke to various studio executives. I spoke to a number of technicians who had been there since the '30s. I even spoke to a woman who claimed to be the unofficial studio historian. None of these people knew anything at all about Frances Farmer except that she had been an enigmatic star who had gone insane and written a book about it. I left Paramount and began calling people who had been in her classes in the old days—Marsha Hunt, Betty Burgess, and one or two others whose names I thought I recognized.

These people did remember Frances Farmer from those days and what they remembered most about her was that she had a difficult time adjusting right from the start. She hated publicity parties and fixed dates and all the other degrading little rituals to which young starlets were expected to subject themselves to get noticed. The indulgence of the place seemed frankly to shock her. In class she was quick and displayed flashes of brilliance, but she was distainful of the whole process of filmmaking. ("I have difficulty considering this acting," she complained after her debut in a Community Chest trailer. "How can anyone possibly build a characterization under these circumstances?") She was so unhappy that she was just about to shuck the entire venture and go back to Seattle when a director spotted her in a test and picked her for the ingenue role in a movie about life in a military school called *Too Many Parents* at the end of January, 1936.

The Seattle press was so excited by the announcement that Frances Farmer, the "bad girl of

West Seattle," was going to star in a Hollywood movie that they sent reporters down to cover the story. Under a grinning page-one picture of Frances, the *Post-Intelligencer* reported:

> The big chance in pictures that Frances Farmer, pretty University of Washington graduate, had yearned for came with Cinderella-like unexpectedness just when she had given up hope of "breaking in."
>
> The Seattle girl . . . had been working as a foil for other players taking screen tests, but could not interest producers in her talent.
>
> Discouraged, she was about to leave the studios and try her luck on the speaking stage.
>
> Then—and it sounds almost like a fairy tale—she was "feeding" dialogue to another aspirant in a test when she attracted the attention of a director. He recognized her ability at once.
>
> As a result, she was given the ingenue lead in the forthcoming picture *Too Many Parents*.
>
> And that is Hollywood!

Parents turned out to be essentially a grade-B filler starring Billy Lee and Carl "Alfalfa" Switzer. It was shot quickly on a shoestring and billed as "a punch-packed human drama of youngsters who make spunk take the place of love their parents forgot to give them." In Seattle it played at the Paramount Theater (the very theater Frances had

61

worked in as an usherette for over two years) amid a lot of publicity about her Moscow trip of a few months before, and people went to see it mainly out of curiosity. Nationally it did well, and when I saw it in a musty West Hollywood screening room ("This thing has not been out of the can in forty years," the projectionist said), it was easy to understand why, Frances was on screen throughout the film and though her lines were almost embarrassingly inane, she was utterly fascinating to watch. Audiences went away remembering *that* face and *that* voice and with the feeling they had seen someone very much on the way up. All things considered, it was quite a successful feature debut, and Paramount promised her better things in the future.

Immediately after the filming of this first movie, Frances made a decision that, in retrospect, was totally out of character with the rest of her life. Whether it was a sudden infatuation or merely because she was lonely and insecure, no one knew, but within the space of week, she somehow convinced herself that she had fallen seriously in love. The man was a fellow Paramount contract student named Wycliffe Anderson, who within the next year would change his name to William Anderson and then again to Glenn Erickson and finally to Leif Erickson. In later years, Erickson would be known as a light leading man in B movies and then a hard-nosed father figure in hundreds of movies and the television series *High Chapparal*. In 1936, he was a tall, blond, childishly enthusiastic man who had been a vocalist with Ted Fio Rito's dance band. Erickson had fallen in love with Frances practically on the spot (as, indeed, who hadn't?). He pursued her relentlessly and finally convinced her they had everything in common. They rehearsed together, dined in out-of-the-way bistros, took midnight automobile rides up the coast, listened to classical music, spent hours analyzing stories and characters from class.

One day in February, 1936—after she had been in Hollywood less than five months—they got in the car, drove to Yuma, Arizona, and were married by a justice of the peace. Up in Seattle, Lillian Farmer called the newspapers and announced the marriage. About Erickson, she said: "He seems like a very fine young man—over the phone anyhow. And I'm sure the marriage is going to be a success. A lot of people don't realize it, but Frances is very domestic. She's a splendid cook and a very capable housekeeper." The next day, Frances told an angry Paramount the unhappy news, moved into a tiny house with her new husband, and set about the very difficult business of trying to become a major movie star.

13

Erickson would not see me. His publicity person told me he did not talk about Frances Farmer. She said it was a terrible tragedy and it happened a "long, long time ago." She said he had suffered from some of the later accounts of her life, in which he was largely blamed. The truth was that he really knew very little about Frances Farmer. They were married for a few years when they were very young and then they separated ("over career differences"), and later she went insane. She was as much a mystery to him as she had been to everyone else.

In any case, after the marriage she went directly into another low-budget production called *Border Flight,* starring John Howard, a quickie melodrama filmed in about ten days ("By long odds the worst picture ever made," she told an interviewer). There appears to be no existing print of this long-forgotten B movie, but she must have been good because she got some decent notices despite the film's generally scathing reviews. She came across so well in both of these first two efforts, in fact, that Paramount decided to take a chance and give her a bigger part in a more important picture that was just going into production, called *Rhythm on the Range.*

Rhythm was one more picture about a runaway heiress who finds love with a common man, a genre that had been rather painfully overworked since the success of *It Happened One Night* three years before. It was directed by Norman Taurog and starred Bing Crosby, Bob Burns, and a very young Martha Raye. It was also a semimusical featuring such songs as "I'm an Old Cowhand," "Rhythm on the Range," and "I Can't Escape You." Frances came across in the film better than anyone had dared to expect. Her patrician beauty and unusual manner of delivery attracted most of the critical attention away from Crosby himself ("Frances Farmer is just a delight!" three different critics wrote), and when the picture turned out to be a huge popular success, one of the film industry's top twenty box-office hits of the year, the upper echelon of Paramount decided to sit back and take a closer look at what they had in Frances Farmer.

By some coincidence, the movie itself turned up on the television late, late show the week I was in Hollywood. I stayed up to 3:45 A.M. to catch it and, despite the hour and the interruption of endless used-car commercials, I was once again captivated by the images of Frances Farmer. The woman seemed to possess a kind of intoxicating screen presence that was impossible to ignore. Her performance here was limited—she was very much kept subordinate to Crosby—but it was still marvelously "right." Even within the confines of playing

65

an ingenue in a musical, she was able to convey a woman of considerable depth and intelligence. Maybe I was seeing more than was actually there, but her presence seemed full of the inner strength and honesty that seemed to characterize everything I had learned about her life so far. Overwhelmed by this screen image, I wondered once again how such a woman could go suddenly insane.

There were certainly no answers to that question from what remained of the cast and crew of *Rhythm on the Range*. I spoke to whomever I could find through the various guilds and they all said they "didn't get to know her." She stayed very much to herself during those first few months and made most of her friends outside the movie crowd. She seemed to get along particularly well with Bing Crosby, who also came from Washington State (and who gave her a beautiful diamond necklace which she cherished for years), but during the shooting of *Rhythm* she began to acquire the reputation for being a rather shy, secretive person who spent the endless idle waits between shots reading and taking long walks by herself. Crosby said she had not quite mastered the technique of film acting, of maintaining a characterization while filming in short, unrelated sequences, and while making the picture she remained in an almost constant state of nervousness that many people took for arrogance. This uncertainty is reflected in nearly every one of her interviews during and after the film: As she said to one interviewer: "I had no idea what the picture was about all the time I was making it. I never did find out. I was just the tall skinny dame while Crosby

66

and Martha Raye and Bob Burns were having the time of their lives. No one from the front office ever even talked to me about my role. It was a long sweet nightmare for me. . . ."

There is not much else to tell about those first few months in Hollywood. By the middle of the year, her life had finally ordered itself into a kind of routine. She worked usually up to ten hours a day at the studio. When she wasn't working on a film, she was either studying or exercising or trying out for parts, which left little time for a home life. She was actually under considerable strain at home (she and Erickson were already not getting along, and her mother—ecstatic at having a movie actress for a daughter—had come down from Seattle to stay in their tiny Laurel Canyon home). After *Rhythm*, she began staying even later at the studio and working even harder. She seemed to think that absolutely anything could be accomplished by hard work and she thrived on the long hours and grinding self-discipline. It was as if her only purpose in life were to prepare herself for that big break which Paramount promised would make everything right.

14

The break came in May, 1936, after Frances
had been in Hollywood only about seven
months. The story goes that Howard Hawks was
looking through a number of tests to cast small parts
for *Come and Get It,* a big-budget epic he was
directing for Samuel Goldwyn, when the rushes of
Rhythm on the Range were screened. He was so excited by what he saw ("That girl has the beauty and
wit to be another Carole Lombard!" he supposedly
shouted) that he arranged to borrow her, not for a
small part but for the plum two-part starring role
that had originally been cast with the actress
Virginia Bruce.

It was, by any measure, a tremendous stroke
of luck for Frances. Based on Edna Ferber's best
seller about two generations of Wisconsin loggers,
the picture was planned to be in every way a "prestige" production and one of Goldwyn's major
releases of the year. Sweeping location sequences
were to be filmed in Washington State by a second
unit under Richard Rossen, while the cast, which
besides Frances included Edward Arnold, Joel
McCrea, and Walter Brennan (he would win the first
Academy Award in the category of Best Supporting

Actor for his performance) shot interiors at the Goldwyn Studios in Hollywood. Hawks was directing from a script by Jules Furthman, and Gregg Toland, the master cinematographer who would later photograph *Citizen Kane,* was behind the camera.

Frances had what was clearly the largest and most important part in the film. She was to play a dual role of a world-weary saloon whore and her virginal daughter, both of whom are loved by the hero (Arnold), a lumber camp boy who becomes a timber tycoon. She felt it was the first time she had been given a chance really to act in a film, and for perhaps the first time since college, she was ecstatically happy and creatively involved in something. She also got along extremely well with her director, Howard Hawks. They would often go out for weekend trips on his boat, and together they prowled the red-light district of Los Angeles to research the mannerisms of prostitutes. Hawks delighted in her fresh-scrubbed beauty and overwhelming sense of dedication, and forty years later he would still get misty-eyed when he spoke about her. "I think," he says utterly without hesitation, "that she had more talent than anyone I ever worked with."

The filming of *Come and Get It* got under way in June and was almost immediately beseiged with problems. The main complication was with the script. In the Ferber novel, the hero becomes infatuated with the daughter of the woman he once loved, only to lose the girl to his own son. This adult theme had disturbed the conservative Goldwyn from the beginning, and he got into bitter disagreements with Hawks over just how to end the film. After production was already well under way, Goldwyn decided that the Ferber ending would have to be changed. Hawks went ahead and wrote several suitable endings himself for Goldwyn to choose from and shot them. Goldwyn became furious with Hawks for tampering with the script without his knowledge, and fired him. Hawks was replaced by William Wyler, who didn't want the job and had to be threatened with suspension before he would accept the contract assignment. Frances had total confidence in Hawks, and his replacement turned out to be very traumatic for her. In the best of times, Wyler was a cold and demanding director who bullied his actors into good performances. Under these circumstances, he was nearly impossible to work with and he made life sheer misery for everyone on the set. "Acting with Wyler is the nearest thing to slavery," she said of the director. "He is a madhouse." "The nicest thing I can say about Frances Farmer," said the direct er of her, "is that she is unbearable."

The pressure on Frances was more than any twenty-one-year-old girl should have had to bear. It was her first starring role and she was expected to hold the picture together single-handedly, to be convincing as two very different types of women, and as a love object to two very different types of men. Walter Brennan, who played both her husband and father in the film, later said that the only way she was able to get through it was by ignoring everything around her and throwing herself totally into the part. She worked day and night during the long and turbulent weeks of filming to sharpen her character-izations to razorlike perfection. Her single-minded determination alienated many of her co-workers (several of whom publicly stated they would never work with her again), but it earned her the respect of Arnold and Brennan, both of whom considered her a major talent.

The picture was finally assembled in cutting room B in the Goldwyn Studios at the end of 1936 by film editor Edward Curtiss. It is said that when Samuel Goldwyn came out of the screening room after viewing the final cut, he had an enormous smile on his face. This girl managed to capture brilliantly both the ennui of the mother and the freshness and hope of the daughter. *Come and Get It* was going to be a giant success and Frances Farmer had stolen the show.

15

It was really quite incredible. People in Seattle could hardly believe it. In less than a year since this girl had scandalized the city by a Communist-sponsored tour of the Soviet Union, she had become a major star at age twenty-one, compared to Hepburn and Garbo ("Frances Farmer will be as great and probably greater than Garbo," Louella Parsons said flatly.) Whatever she had done or been in the past, she was now a major public figure, and the Chamber of Commerce was suddenly willing to let bygones be bygones and embrace her with open arms. ("The old hometown, which has adopted Frances Farmer as its own, to laud or criticize as old hometowns will do when somebody's daughter gets famous, should be proud of her," the *Seattle Times* editorialized.)

The world premiere of *Come and Get It* was held in Seattle's Liberty Theater and a lavish reception was given at the Olympic Hotel, the city's finest, with Washington Governor Clarence Martin himself there to pay tribute to Frances Farmer, the "Cinderella girl" of Seattle. She spoke before a huge assembly at the University of Washington, and she and her parents (united for the occasion) were guests of honor at a student production of *A Doll's House*. She was driven through the business district in a limousine, and crowds lined the streets to catch a glimpse of her. The Seattle press covered her every movement, playing the whole affair as the greatest true-life fairy tale in the history of the Northwest. "She has left as an outcast," said one enthusiastic radio commentator, "and come back a star!"

Frances, however, did not accept the role of Cinderella graciously. She was unwilling to play the prodigal daughter returning in triumph. She refused to autograph copies of *Come and Get It* at the Bon Marché ("I didn't write the book, you know). She shocked reporters with her sarcastic answers and irritated city officials with her haughty manner ("Remember me?" she asked one leading minister. "I'm the freak from West Seattle High.") The noted *Life* magazine journalist Paul O'Neil, who as a young reporter for the *Seattle Times,* covered her return as one of the biggest news stories of the year, pointed out the irony of the situation:

> Frances Farmer, former University of Washington coed, who left Seattle on a bus in 1935 to see the wide world, and to seek her fortune, came home last night in a transport airplane, as befitted a star of moving pictures.
>
> Many things, some of them hardly conceivable, had happened to her. In less than a year she had become a sort of Cinderella in the

eyes of moving picture fans. Her name had blossomed in lights on the marquees of the nation's theaters. . . .

Frances Farmer, who always did and said about as she pleased when she was a coed, did it again, and was, bless her heart, a little disconcerting to her setting.

Faced with the hardest of hard jobs, coming back to the old hometown a success, she climbed off the plane, looking, talking, and acting exactly as she did when she climbed on the bus for a trip to Russia.

Although she had found fame and fortune on the return trip by way of New York and Hollywood, she might have been climbing out of an automobile after a shopping trip.

She wore no makeup, save a little lipstick; she wore a coat which could have been worn on the campus on a rainy day, and she had her own eyebrows.

"They did all sorts of things to me in New York, when I had my screen test," she said. "They shaved off my eyebrows . . . and they cut my hair, gave me a permanent wave and experimented with makeup. . . .

"But when I got to Hollywood, they didn't seem to notice me so much, and I finally got my eyebrows back. I've been trying to be natural ever since and I'm beginning to succeed, I think."

Did she ever feel she was "going Hollywood"? She didn't know about that. She said that she and her husband—she was married in February to a young actor named William Anderson—lived in a shack, kept three dogs, and got up early to go to work.

She talked directly, frankly, and at times with a touch of sarcasm.

There seemed to be something "vaguely insulting" about the way she responded to questions, about her fierce independence and indifference to popular opinion, and it was implied in all the stories about her. Her friends who were at the strange homecoming say she had a genuine contempt for all these people who now wanted to shake her hand. These were the same respectable citizens who had castigated her for her "godless" essay and who wanted to string her up for her trip to Russia. These politicians and civic leaders were, many of them, the American Vigilantes of Washington, and she hated everything they stood for. When one right-wing Congressman introduced himself to her at the reception, she called him a "hypocrite" and calmly walked away.

16

After the disastrous homecoming premiere of *Come and Get It,* Frances flew back down to Hollywood and quickly made three more movies —one on loan to RKO and two for Paramount. These pictures were all very popular, with big budgets and big-name co-stars, and yet they are almost never shown anymore. A man in the Paramount projection room told me that these films literally had not been screened "in years." He said that even though they had all been highly successful, for some reason—probably because Frances Farmer had gone crazy and the company was embarrassed about it—most of the prints had been withdrawn from circulation sometime in the early '40s.

The first of these was *Toast of New York,* in which she played opposite Cary Grant and Edward Arnold. Based on Matthew Josephson's book *The Robber Barons,* it was a highly fictionalized version of the life of "Big Jim" Fisk and his mistress Josie Mansfield, who together were the scandal of Wall Street in the 1860s. The film was marvelous entertainment, with Grant and Arnold almost perfect as the financial con men and stunning art direction by Van Nest Polgaste. Frances sang a song called "The

First Time I Saw You" (which became a modest hit in late 1937), and sang and danced her way through a lavish musical montage sequence. As Josie, she gave a tight and convincing performance of a woman torn between two strong men, and she received excellent reviews. Roland V. Lee, the director, recalls that Frances had done an enormous amount of historical research on the character and had wanted to play her as a very strong-willed whore. The studio preferred a milder interpretation, however, and shooting was held up for days while they argued about it. ("I don't understand," she would say over and over again. "I just don't understand why you want to plaster sweetening over the character when it's so much more interesting to tell the truth.") Frances finally had to give in, and consequently she ended up hating her association with the film, which is a shame since her performance holds up very well over the years.

Before the end of the shooting of *Toast,* she had already started filming a second major feature called *Ebb Tide.* This one was a moody South Sea adventure filmed almost entirely on the Paramount back lot by an undistinguished director named James Hogan. Based on a story by Robert Louis Stevenson, it was a tale of three beachcombers (Oscar Homolka, Barry Fitzgerald, and Ray Milland) who steal a ship, encounter a beautiful stowaway (Frances), and stop at an island where they have a confrontation with a religious fanatic (Lloyd Nolan). It was a strange and confusing story shot in gaudy Technicolor by cameramen Leo Tover and Ray Rennahan. Once again, Frances is said to have rebelled at her part ("an ill-defined bit of nothing," she called it) and once again she came across magnificently—an almost painfully sumptuous and enigmatic figure—and the picture made money and boosted her career.

The last film to come out of this flurry of activity (once again begun before the last one was finished) was a rather typical newspaper melodrama called *Exclusive,* directed with a cynical flourish by Alexander Hall. Frances plays the daughter of an aging reporter (Charlie Ruggles) who is in love with an idealistic younger reporter (Fred MacMurray), and together they battle the take-over of their paper by a gangster (Lloyd Nolan). Frances had been called in as a last-minute replacement for Carole Lombard and she didn't like the script, which called for a "newspaperwoman who has to give expression to all the class A human emotions; who has to be happy, then tearful; gentle as a cooing dove and then hard as nails." She had been associated with journalism long enough to know how absurd the whole story was, but this time she didn't put up a fight. She turned in a light and likable performance and made a particularly strong romantic team with MacMurray, and the picture was yet another big success.

During this period, it was as if she could do no wrong. Every film she touched seemed to turn to gold. She was now—along with Lombard, Colbert, and Dietrich—one of the top female stars in Paramount's stable. The front office was planning various projects to star her opposite Gary Cooper, Ronald Coleman, and (on loan to M-G-M) Clark Gable. (It was even said that old Adolph Zukor, the

78

head and founder of Paramount, had become personally enchanted with her, that he wanted to personally push her career.) Since she was only twenty-two years old and just beginning to scratch the surface of her potential, it was almost taken for granted around the lot that she would one day be the biggest female star in American films.

17

And yet, while Frances was grinding out these three successive films in the early days of 1937, she began to emerge gradually—once again in her life—as a very controversial figure. The people who knew her at the time say that her attitude and feelings about Hollywood underwent a complete transformation. They say that she suddenly looked around one morning and could see nothing but shallowness and deceit. In retrospect, of course, one can recognize that she had not changed at all—it was merely that same passionate honesty and stubborn independence of the essay-winning little girl of West Seattle reasserting itself once again. But at the time it took Hollywood very much by surprise. While she had always been uncompromising in her dealings with the studio (she had, for instance, withstood great pressure to change her name), she now seemed eager to take on all the sham and hypocrisy of Hollywood single-handedly.

She adamantly refused to make any concessions to stardom or compromises in the way she lived. She would not wear makeup or have her hair done professionally. She shocked studio publicists by using language that a lady should not even know

80

existed. (Her favorite all-purpose word was *cock-sucker*.) In June, she offended her hometown and her alma mater, the University of Washington, by telling a delegation of visiting drama students that, frankly, a university education was worthless to an actress. She drove an old wreck of a car and lived with her husband in a house that was, in her own words, little more than a shack. She dressed sloppily and refused interviews and generally did not give a damn what anyone thought of her, much as a generation of young stars would do several decades later. Hollywood correspondent Kyle Crichton wrote of her at the time:

> She is a tall, thin girl who is more intelligent-looking than beautiful, uses no makeup off the set, doesn't give a damn for clothes, is going to be an actress if Hollywood will let her, and is going back this summer to play in a stock company in Seattle, and don't anybody get the notion she won't do it. Her taste in clothes is atrocious because there is nothing in the world she cares less about. She likes sailing, is not particularly athletic, thinks movie gossip is blah ... and will give up all salary boosts ever heard of if they'll give her decent pictures to play in. She is married to Leif Erickson, the movie actor, and they live in a canyon home which will never be photographed as a showplace and can be reached only by a mountain guide equipped with a divining rod. The second-hand roadster is getting feebler and faintly

81

less green by the year and she was cursed soundly by a few hundred motorists on Melrose Avenue no later than last February when the engine died and she was out pushing the thing to safety.

During the filming of *Toast of New York*, *Collier's* magazine sent Crichton out to do a long profile of her. Paramount was extremely nervous about the interview because of her controversial girlhood (the Russian trip had always been referred to in her official biography as "a prize won in a local popularity contest"), and gave her all sorts of instructions on what to say and what not to say. When Frances sat down with the reporter, she told the entire candid story of her life, omitting nothing—including the wonders she had witnessed in the Soviet Union. The story was published under the title "I Dress as I Like" and it was in effect her written declaration of war against the false image Hollywood was trying to impose on her.

Not long after that, she began to become identified again with a number of left-wing political causes. Many of her old friends had filtered down to Hollywood by this time (her old pal Sophie Rosenstein was among the first, and Sophie's husband—a former hat salesman named Arthur Weinstein—became Frances' business manager), and largely through them, she had become part of a radical circle of friends. She began doing volunteer work for various peace organizations and groups supporting the Loyalists in the Spanish Civil War. The involvement was so exhilarating for her that she was soon spending all of her spare time away from the studio working for radical causes.

This political involvement was an almost perfect outlet for someone with Frances' idealistic temperament and driving energy. Her favorite cause was a movement to improve the plight of California's growing number of migrant farm workers. She drove out to the San Joaquin Valley with a group of radical friends and was so horrified at the living and working conditions of the laborers that she vowed to do something about it. She came back to Hollywood and immediately set about organizing rallies and making speeches and harassing stars and producers into contributing to the cause. She was so moved by the pathetic state of the workers, in fact, that she donated not only time and effort but (as would come out several years later in legal proceedings) enormous amounts of her own money in their behalf.

To learn this, I spent nearly a month searching out former '30s radicals in the backstreets of Hollywood. Nearly twenty-five years after the end of McCarthyism, these people were still reluctant to talk about their involvement in those days—genuinely frightened, it would seem, of some new wave of political repression. But they all seemed to have Frances Farmer stories and they all seemed to remember her as an important figure—an incorruptible and romantic radical heroine who had actually been to Mother Russia and hobnobbed with the Politburo. Her assocation with radical politics is one of the great forgotten stories of '30s Hollywood, and somebody at Paramount did a consummate job of covering it up. Forty years later few people would remember it, but in 1937, Frances Farmer was the most stubborn, uncompromising, unconventional star Hollywood had ever seen.

18

Everything I had learned about Frances Farmer seemed to lead to another question and heighten the mystery surrounding her. If, for instance, she had been one of Paramount's biggest box-office stars in '36 and '37, why was there no mention of her name in any of the official histories of the studio? If she were such a commanding figure of Hollywood radical politics, why had no account of that fact survived in the dozens of books written on the subject? If she were to go violently insane within a few short years, why was there not a single clue to it in her behavior in this period? I had been searching for quite a few months now and still had no satisfactory answers.

Frances left Hollywood and went East in the summer of 1937. She had been there little more than a year and, after her dazzling success, she apparently decided that the time had come to get out of that crazy town and fulfill her long-standing ambition to become a great stage actress. Despite the opposition of Paramount and the disapproval of practically everyone she knew, she got leave from her contract, left her husband in Laurel Canyon, and accepted two offers to act in summer stock on

85

the East Coast—C. K. Munro's comedy *At Mrs. Beams's* with Mildred Natwick at the Mount Kisco Playhouse in Westchester County, New York, the first week of August, and *The Petrified Forest* with Phillips Holmes later in the month at Westport, Connecticut.

She would later say that these two engagements turned out to be the most satisfying experience of her entire career. The weeks she spent in rural Connecticut were like the first happy vacation she had had since college. She worked very hard in rehearsals and turned in two altogether admirable performances—especially at Westport, where she got rave reviews. After seeing her debut, critic Douglas Gilbert wrote:

> Her regular features are as frank as a dollar watch and a superb indication of her attitude. She has no illusions about her talent, freely admitting that what she knows about the art of the legitimate stage is molecular and, that using her hard-won studio vacation to make these arduous summer appearances, is simply for study and practice.

The Mount Kisco staff remember her as a "dream" to work with, in fact so cooperative and pleasant that both theaters were begging her to return for the next season if she could swing it with Paramount. "I have never known how much I hated picture making until I got away from it," she wrote the staff in appreciation. "How wonderful it is to be able to build and carry a characterization without studio interference or some nitwit director forever screaming 'Cut' at you! More than ever I am convinced that I belong body and soul to the theater."

This determination to turn her back on Hollywood and develop as an actress seemed to have earned her the admiration of the Eastern press, and for the first time in her career favorable stories began appearing (most of them quoting her at length criticizing the "vulgarity" of Hollywood). *Vogue* did a major picture spread with a commentary that gushed with compliments:

> "The find since Garbo," wrote the movie critics about Frances Farmer, but "the most promising young dramatic talent the movies have developed in a long time," wrote the dramatic critics. Possessed of a beautiful profile, an unorthodox sense of timing, and a quality of fresh lucidity, she bolted to success. Two years ago, her career had only involved working her way through college, a trip to Moscow—won in a newspaper popularity contest—and a screen test. Since then, she has played in seven pictures, indulged her child's love of dressing up (she used to try on Dietrich's old costumes down in the wardrobe room), and now hates to dress for evening. This summer she came East, without hurrah, to make her debut on the legitimate stage at the Westchester Playhouse....

Such publicity did much to counter her bad press

on the West Coast and also quickly put her in demand in New York theatrical circles.

She suddenly found herself an immensely popular figure. The theater people who met her were overwhelmed by her quick wit, keen intellect, and dazzling beauty, and years later would remember her with almost the exact same words: "I loved her!" The actor Henry Morgan, who at the time was just getting started in New York and who came to know her quite well (Frances later introduced him to his wife), recalled her as "warm and wonderful." He said, "There was no one more healthy looking, radiant, and alive than Frances. People loved being around her ... she was so much fun. I don't know anyone who disliked her during this time. She was just a goddess."

After the *Vogue* layout, she got a call from Harold Clurman, director of the famous New York Group Theater. Clurman had met her once briefly at a rally for American volunteers to fight in the Spanish Civil War and he had secretly attended one of her stock performances. He liked her politics and he thought she was an extraordinary young actress. He invited her up to his Manhattan apartment, offered her a cocktail, and point-blank asked her to join the Group. "Clifford Odets has written a play," he said. "It's called *Golden Boy* and I think you'd be right for the feminine lead." It was the very thing she had worked toward all her adult life and she leaped at the chance.

19

The Group Theater had originated in the early '30s as an experimental theatrical group dedicated to the artistic principles of the Russian master Stanislavsky, as taught by two former members of the Moscow Art Theater named Richard Boleslavsky and Maria Ouspenskaya. It soon acquired a politically radical, left-wing orientation and became famous for such "activist" plays as Clifford Odets' *Waiting for Lefty* and *Awake and Sing*. The Group finally expired at the end of the Depression, a victim of its own success and the affluence of its members (it was succeeded by the Actors Studio, which followed the same principles in a somewhat less political manner), but at the time Frances was fascinated with it. Its name was synonymous with everything that was art in the theater.

Frances joined the Group to do *Golden Boy* at the end of September, 1937. She was to play Lorna Moon, a "tough young tramp from Newark" who convinces sensitive, violin-playing Joe Bonaparte (Luther Adler) first to take up and then give up prizefighting. She worked harder than she had ever worked in her life, and soon won over a

89

resentful cast which included such future luminaries as Lee J. Cobb, John Garfield, Elia Kazan, Martin Ritt, Howard Da Silva, and Karl Malden. After months of rehearsal, the play opened in November to rave reviews and went on to become a modern American classic and the biggest financial success the Group would ever have.

Frances' performance was singled out as the finest thing in the play. Her notices were the best of her career. *Life* Magazine did a major feature on her, illustrated with a full-page progression of pictures depicting the "amazing Cinderella story" of the Seattle girl who had conquered Hollywood and now Broadway at the tender age of twenty-three:

When Frances Farmer was a young tomboy in a Seattle high school, she once lost a debate because the judges thought she was too dramatic. So Frances decided to be an actress. She set about learning to act with all the energy her dynamic, logical, and earnest personality could muster. Beautiful looks gave her leads in college productions where she learned something. A newspaper popularity contest took her to Moscow where she learned more. A screen test took her to Hollywood where her photogenic face with its fine forehead and high cheekbones promptly converted her into a fledgling star. But after seven pictures (including *Come and Get It* and *Toast of New York*), Frances Farmer felt there was more to be learned about acting than Hollywood could teach her. This feeling

90

took her to a summer theater, then to Broadway. . . . Autograph fans now line up nightly
outside her stage door in the belief she will
become one of moviedom's brighter stars.

Night after night it was the same thing. Everyone of
importance in New York wanted to meet her. Stars
the caliber of Spencer Tracy and Bing Crosby
pushed their way through the crowd to get back-
stage. Old friends from Seattle came to share in the
triumph. (Her high school teacher Belle McKenzie
was there, and like everyone else she was knocked
out by Frances' performance.) Broadway autograph
seekers and newspaper reporters followed her
wherever she went. "The world," wrote one
Broadway columnist, "is literally at this young girl's
feet."

Frances was thoroughly, happily, ecstatically
satisfied with her success. There had been some
minor disappointments, to be sure; there had been,
in fact, little of the honesty and purity she had expected to find in the Group Theater—she had found
instead all the bickering and backbiting and destructive vanity she had so detested in the film industry.
And the Group actors, far from being the artistic
purists she had always believed them to be, all
seemed to want to go to Hollywood and make piles
of money (which, eventually, most of them did).
But she was thrilled at being part of this famous
group of theater professionals and she could be
content with the knowledge that she had accomplished everything she had set out to do when she left
Seattle.

91

Back in Seattle, however, the success of *Golden Boy* was having a somewhat different effect. In a single evening, Frances Farmer had become the most important artist ever to come out of the Northwest and she had done it in a left-wing play performed by a "Communist" theater group. It was, suddenly, the essay and the Russian trip all over again. Her mother was terribly upset by her connection with the Group Theater. The same city officials who had welcomed her after *Come and Get It* were shocked and embarrassed that she would leave Hollywood and work for peanuts with this nefarious organization. One of the leaders of the American Vigilantes of Washington was so angry he publicly vowed they would get even "if it were the last thing they ever did."

20

While I was researching Frances' involvement with the Group Theater, I wrote a long newspaper article raising certain questions about the mysterious fate of Frances Farmer. After the article appeared, I went on one of those radio talk shows in which listeners phone in their comments. I did not anticipate the response I received from all this. Over the following weeks, I was deluged with calls and letters from people who claimed to have known her in every stage of her life. All these people seemed to have tantalizing little bits of information, stories, anecdotes, rumors, letters, to give me and they all somehow believed there must be something very wrong about the commitment of Frances Farmer.

One person who did not think there was anything wrong in the commitment was a woman in Portland, Oregon, who said she was Frances' older sister Edith. She wrote me a strange and bitter letter about this time, which I was surprised to receive, since I had been told by two neighbors that she was not living (what they had actually meant, it later turned out, was that Edith was not living "in the city"). She had read my article and was extremely upset about it. She said that the autobio-

93

graphy and everything else ever written about her sister were "lies." She said that the truth would come out someday and she would be the one to present it. Then she wrote my editor and threatened to sue if I didn't quit poking my nose into her "family business."

I wrote her back and, over a period of months, we began a regular correspondence. She seemed to me very hostile and suspicious at first—she maintained she had been badly stung by newspaper reporters in her time—and there were many areas about which she absolutely refused to speak. She had been living in Hawaii during most of her sister's tragedy and it occurred to me that exactly what had *really* happened was as much a mystery to her as it was to me—though she was quite sure she had the truth. Her theory, briefly stated, is that the Communists drove Frances crazy. She seemed particularly bitter toward the Group Theater and its left-wing members, who, she said, took criminal advantage of Frances' kind nature and then harassed her into insanity. Whether or not there was any truth to this I could not say at that point, but it was obvious that a whole swarm of troubles began for Frances immediately after the success of *Golden Boy*.

No sooner was the play firmly established as a hit, in fact, than Shepard Traube, the New York agent who had originally signed her up, sued for nonpayment on his personal contract, demanding $75,000, a figure representing 10 percent of her earnings up to that time. (He charged that he had spotted her picture in the newspaper just before the

94

Russian trip, sought her out, and brought her to the attention of Paramount, and was therefore entitled to continuing compensation as her manager.) Traube had not acted in her behalf since she signed the Paramount contract, which she had been advised (by Paramount) invalidated her relationship with him. She had not even seen the man since 1935. She went to court at the end of June, 1938, and, after several weeks of intense struggle, finally had the charges dismissed on a technicality. Supreme Court Justice Samuel I. Rosenman ruled that Traube "did not have the necessary theatrical employment license, which is required even in an isolated contract with one person.... His sole service was in connection with employment and not managing the defendant." But it had been an exhausting battle that drained her of money, time, and sorely needed energy.

While this case was dragging through the courts in New York, another problem was brewing back in Hollywood. It seemed that everyone on the Coast abhorred Frances' involvement with the Group Theater—her agents, her family, most of all Paramount Studios, who considered it an unnecessary drain on her earning potential. The leave from her contract was only for the New York run of the play and when that ended around the middle of the year, Paramount called her back to Hollywood and cast her in a minor adventure film called *Escape from Yesterday* (released as *Ride a Crooked Mile*), directed by Alfred E. Green and starring Akim Tamiroff and her husband, Leif Erickson, from whom she had been more or less estranged.

When Frances read the script, she couldn't believe it. It was a corny, cliché-ridden B picture about a Russian Cossack turned cattle rustler and his attempts to reform. Her part (as a cafe singer) was clearly a supporting role in which she was required to stand on the sidelines and mouth a lot of maudlin dialogue. The film was her punishment for all the critical remarks she had made about Hollywood in the Eastern press, and the studio executives did not even try to disguise the fact. She had treated Paramount badly—Zukor himself had been displeased—and they were going to put her back in line or she could go on indefinite suspension.

Frances stalled around for several weeks trying to decide what to do. It was a dilemma which seemed to have no solution. On the one hand, she had had a giant Broadway success, a triumph which needed to be followed up with a quality film and which, she rightly felt, could be totally negated by a potboiler like *Escape*. On the other, if she followed her instincts and refused to do the film, she would almost certainly receive a year's suspension and that too would kill the interest and momentum generated by *Golden Boy*. In the end, she decided to do the picture without complaining, but only because Erickson convinced her he needed the starring role to boost his career.

Soon after the principal photography of *Escape* was finished, the Farmer family had its first reunion in ten years at the home of Frances' half sister Rita Farmer Smith (the daughter by Lillian's first marriage) in Venice, California. Lillian Farmer had just returned from a year-long trip around the world (a gift from Frances), E. M. Farmer had taken a train down from Seattle, Edith Farmer had come over from Hawaii (where she was working as a home economist for the Hilo Gas and Electric Company), and Wesley Farmer was on leave from the army (where he was a career officer). Frances and Leif Erickson also attended, and it would be one of the last times they would ever appear together as a couple.

Frances went to Chicago and rejoined the *Golden Boy* cast for a ten-week road-show tour, but her heart was no longer in it. She had apparently lost all affection for Erickson by this time and she was feeling terribly empty and lonely. While in Chicago, she had a brief, one-night affair with a businessman much older than herself. It was a casual enough affair and yet it was her first such experience and she felt enormous guilt. Many times in the following months she would confess this transgression to various friends and it would seem to serve as a kind of symbolic act of divorce for her.

When the road-show tour ended in Washington, D.C., Frances kicked off a refugee relief drive with much fanfare at the Spanish embassy and then went back to New York and directly into rehearsals for Irwin Shaw's *Quiet City*, under the direction of her *Golden Boy* costar, Elia Kazan. With only a few weeks of rehearsal to prepare it, the Group Theater production opened to generally unfavorable reviews. Those few who saw *Quiet City* say Frances was not bad in it, but her focus as an actress—her impeccable sense of timing—was clearly off. Kazan says she was upset by personal problems—the troubles with Paramount, a certain loss of faith in herself, the months of legal battling —and her performance simply wasn't all it could or should have been.

21

The failure of *Quiet City* was the first setback of Frances' career and could reasonably have been a deep personal crisis. She seemed to take the failure quite well, however. To regain her confidence, she decided to try a number of smaller and less risky projects. She did some radio broadcasts (most notably *Women in White* with Luther Adler on the *Kate Smith Dramatic Hour*) until summer and then did a few weeks of what she always enjoyed most, summer stock, in suburban New Jersey. Around the first of July, 1939, she and Erickson took a few weeks of vacation at the family home in Seattle.

When she felt that her confidence had been sufficiently restored, she went into another Group Theater production, Robert Ardrey's *Thunder Rock*, with Lee J. Cobb, Franchot Tone, and Luther Adler in the cast. Erickson had also joined the Group Theater by this time and while the two of them were driving to New York for rehearsals, Frances suddenly and inexplicably confessed her one-night affair in Chicago. Erickson was terribly hurt and when they got to the Group's rented estate at Smithtown, Long Island, the couple announced to the world that they were officially separating.

To compensate for this emotional turmoil, Frances threw herself headlong into the play. She strained to do something novel, but she was never able to make much out of her part—a ghost who convinces an isolationist lighthouse keeper to get back into the world's affairs. *Variety* reported succintly that Frances Farmer "flounders hopelessly." After a long rehearsal period and a promising opening night, the play closed within three weeks, another flop.

This second failure just about convinced her to get away from the Group Theater for a while. She had actually been growing weary of the political aspect of her relationship with the Group for some time. It seemed that she was forever being carted around by them to make political statements about the Spanish Civil War and denounce the Dies Committee, which was investigating un-American activities, and although she supported these sentiments in principle, her natural independence balked at the idea of anyone putting words in her mouth. She felt that the Group was more interested in politics than theater, and it began to gnaw at her that she had given them large amounts of money which she knew were not being used for theatrical purposes. When she announced her intentions of leaving, Clifford Odets, the leader of the Group, descended upon her and tried to get her to change her mind.

The Group Theater, which had had dire financial difficulties almost from its inception, could not afford to lose Frances Farmer. *Golden Boy* was the only real hit in the Group's history and Frances Farmer the only real star in its company. Moreover, it had become dependent on the large amounts of Hollywood money she had been feeding into it since 1937. Odets, who had helped found the Group in 1930, an egotistical man ("I am the most talented young playwright in the business," he once told a reporter) with almost unbounded confidence, began pursuing her romantically. Frances was separated, vulnerable, susceptible, and she had long been attracted to him—from the moment she laid eyes on him at the Group party just before leaving for Russia he had represented everything that was pure and honest in the theater to her. He began taking her out and very soon they were having an affair. She moved into his apartment and, according to almost everyone who knew her at the time, she quite simply fell madly, head over heels in love with the man.

The affair was one of the most curious romantic episodes in both their lives. Odets' biographers say he had frankly not expected Frances to fall so hard for him and the depth of her devotion seemed to frighten him. There was also a genuine cruel streak in his character where women were concerned, particularly women who happened to be movie stars. He had been obsessed with Hollywood all his life: his main theme as a playwright was of how a materialistic, success-worshiping world destroys the soul. In his work, Hollywood was the symbol of everything evil in American society, and yet in his personal life he was hopelessly, fatally attracted to it. He was constantly in romantic pursuit

101

of movie stars (he was married to Luise Rainer at the time of his affair with Frances), and would eventually end up in Hollywood grinding out one hack script after another. He was attracted to Frances because she was a film star and he seemed to hate her for the same reason. After she agreed to stay with the Group, he bitterly turned on her, took to humiliating her in public, and finally rejected her entirely—suggesting she go back to Erickson.

The end of the affair almost devastated Frances. It was more than the end of a love affair; it was the abrupt end of all her girlhood illusions about the world of the theater. She simply couldn't understand Odets' sudden change of heart—she wrote countless letters begging for an explanation—and she had a very difficult time accepting the fact that everything was over between them. She had contracted to star in a play by Ernest Hemingway about the Spanish Civil War, called *The Fifth Column*—a Theater Guild production directed by Lee Strasberg and employing mostly Group members. But by the time rehearsals were to start, she was still so upset over Odets that she couldn't bear to go through with it.

When she didn't show up for rehearsals and offered no satisfactory explanations, she immediately received an avalanche of bad publicity. Actor's Equity fined her $1,500. Members of the Group Theater—which had a large financial stake in this particular production—called day and night and harassed her. (Her sister Edith insists they even threatened her with anonymous phone calls.) The play was finally recast with Katherine Locke and

102

because of other problems never got on the boards, but Frances was blamed for its destruction and the publicity almost irreparably damaged her reputation in New York.

22

The months following the collapse of *The Fifth Column* are the most difficult of her career to trace today. Because she stayed very much to herself, there is very little record of what she was thinking and feeling during this time. For those who want to hear such things, there are still a hundred different rumors circulating around Hollywood and New York about Frances Farmer during those months. Reliable people have told me with straight faces that (1) she had become a hopeless drunk; (2) she was having an affair with Howard Hughes; (3) she had become a confirmed Lesbian (this rumor— probably based on the rather mannish quality of her voice—followed her all her life, though I could never substantiate it); (4) she was becoming more deeply involved with Communist sedition; and (5) she was having a succession of abortions (she had, in fact, at least one, probably at the beginning of her marriage).

The truth, at least as I was able to make it out, is not nearly so exciting. She seems merely to have gone into retreat, catching her breath, as it were, before embarking on another big career push. She had undergone a very bad time in New York

104

but she was through crying about it. It is true that she was becoming more argumentative and visibly more high-strung and that she was drinking more than usual, but mainly she was angry and disappointed at her failure. She was going to show people that she could bounce back from adversity and she was going to do it, first of all, by reestablishing herself in Hollywood.

After a short trip to Seattle to visit her mother, she went back to Hollywood and immediately began work on a South Sea adventure for United Artists called *South of Pago Pago*, costarring Jon Hall and Victor McLaglen and directed by her most frequent director in Hollywood, Alfred E. Green. It was perhaps the most consistently awful script she had ever been handed—worse even than *Escape from Yesterday*—but this time she didn't object at all. She came to work every day on time, kept very much to herself, and, in a quiet way, seemed to enjoy the challenge of creating an interesting character out of nothing.

As soon as *South of Pago Pago* was in the can, she went directly to Warner Brothers for another loan-out, a Rex Beach oil-field drama called *Flowing Gold*. The story of two itinerent oil workers who both fall in love with the beautiful daughter of their boss, it was again directed by Alfred Green and starred Pat O'Brien and John Garfield. The studio had not wanted to use Frances in the plum part, but Garfield, a good friend who had been in the *Golden Boy* cast, persuaded them at the last minute. The film turned out to be reasonably successful—and Frances had never photographed more beautifully—but, on the set, she got into one argument after another. It was also the most grueling physical experience of her career—full of long outdoor scenes sloshing around the mud of Warner's Calabasas Ranch—and she became bitterly convinced that Green was ordering endless retakes of her face-down mud scene just to humiliate her.

After the principal photography of *Flowing Gold* was finished, she went back East to reestablish herself in the theater. She did *Little Women* and *Our Betters* (with Constance Collier) at the Cape Playhouse in Dennis, Massachusetts, and then went on to New York for the winter. She looked up some of her old Broadway friends and generally tried to get back in the theatrical crowd. But nothing had changed in the past few months and she was not greeted warmly in New York. Her reputation was still suffering from the *Fifth Column* experience—people were saying the Group Theater had fallen apart because of it—and she was largely ignored by the same people who had once idolized her. This rejection came as a surprise, and she didn't know how to react. She went to a few plays by herself and wandered around Times Square, and then, one gray winter day, she impulsively decided to get out of the city.

She spent the next two weeks driving through the back roads of New England. The experience was so therapeutic that she eventually spent several months of early 1941 traveling around the country, totally incognito, often wearing a black wig. No one knows what she did or felt or even exactly where she went on this mysterious journey across America, but it seems to have turned out to be a positive experience. It was the first time she had done anything on her own—the first time she had had any real rest—since her Russian trip of four years before. She came back refreshed and eager to go back to work and ready for another go at Hollywood. Over and over again in later years—whenever her life became intolerable—she would try to repeat this pleasant, solitary experience. And she would never quite make it.

23

She returned to Hollywood in early April, 1941. She rented the beautiful Malibu beach house that had once belonged to Dolores del Rio and prepared herself to go back to work. She closed herself off with her books and poetry and took long walks on the beach and read far into the nights. She later told an interviewer that she also started an autobiographical novel during this time called *God's Peculiar Care* (the manuscript of which was later destroyed in a fire), and it helped rekindle her high school ambition of becoming a writer. There was (once again) a brief, traumatic visit from her mother, and at the end of the month she went back to work with new energy and made three more movies in quick succession.

I flew back to Hollywood to view the production of this last flurry of creative activity in her life. In a tiny television station screening room I spent one whole afternoon looking at recut 16mm versions of these long-forgotten movies. The first was a screwball comedy with John Barrymore called *World Premiere*, directed by Ted Tetzlaff. The second was a grim little B picture called *Among the Living*, which she made to fulfill the

108

final obligation of her Paramount contract (and which, ironically, is about insanity and a man falsely accused of it). The last one was a big-budget Universal Western called *Badlands of Dakota*, in which she played Calamity Jane to Richard Dix's Wild Bill Hickok.

In each of these films, Frances looked stunning and turned in an excellent movie-star performance. And yet there was something intangibly different about her, a kind of sadness and fatigue— perhaps even desperation—in her eyes that was not there before. I left the screening room and began calling people who had worked with her in these films. Several of them said she was destroying herself with overwork and she was angry and disillusioned because it was getting her nowhere. Susan Hayward, who appeared with her in *Among the Living*, said she had also come to realize how unpopular her outspokenness had made her in this town and to accept the fact that nothing was going to change her bad press. (Louella Parsons: "The highbrow Frances Farmer, who found Hollywood so beneath her a few years ago, is playing, of all things, Calamity Jane.")

After she finished these three pictures, she seemed to vanish again. For several months no one in Hollywood had the slightest idea where she was or what she was doing. There were rumors of all sorts of crazy and irrational exploits during these mysterious lost months (rumors which would later be used against her), but again the truth is mundane: she had simply gone on a much needed vacation. If anyone had cared to check, they would have found that she had actually sat down with a Seattle reporter named Walter Rue a month or so after she finished *Badlands* and given him an in-depth interview. In this interview she revealed exactly what she was doing during this period and there was nothing mysterious about it.

She had worked so hard during the last half of 1941 that the strain was beginning to get to her again. She began to grow tired and irritable and she suffered terrible headaches on the set. After *Badlands* was finished, she got into her car and headed up the coast. Instead of going to Seattle, she veered left at the Washington border and drove most of the way around the remote and rugged Olympic Peninsula, deep in Olympic National Park, to the rustic little resort area of Sol Duc Hot Springs, where years ago she had often gone camping with her father. There, she rented a cabin, hiked among the evergreens, and relaxed for a few days. When she felt herself sufficiently at ease, she called her mother ("Oh, I just got a notion to do a little hiking," she told her) and drove to Seattle.

The very next day, she granted the personal interview to Rue. He wrote that he drove out to West Seattle and found the Farmers in a cozy family setting. Mr. Farmer was reading the paper, Mrs. Farmer was looking through the family album, and Frances was curled up in a chair in front of the big stone fireplace. "I drove up alone from Hollywood by car," she told him, "and when I got to Portland I read in the newspaper about Secretary of the Interior Ickes spending a vacation on the Peninsula.

110

Reading about the Peninsula brought back fond memories for me, so I headed straight for Sol Duc. I stayed there long enough to do a bit of hiking, then came home." She leaned back in the chair and sighed. "You can't imagine what a treat it is to come home like this after a long stretch of picture making and stock performances."

She discussed ("with enthusiasm") her latest films. About *World Premiere* she laughed and said: "In that one I'm a temperamental actress who wears a black wig and tries to look exotic. You should see me!" She spoke about *Among the Living* and *Badlands of Dakota* ("Both were challenging in different ways"). She spoke about her family ("When I return to Hollywood I'm going to take my mother with me and have her stay for a long visit"). And she spoke about her separation from Leif Erickson, which she said was complete and final ("There's no new romance either. I'm too busy with my work to bother about such things").

The interview—and her state of mind during it—are important because sometime later testimony would be taken that at this point Frances was running off to the mountains and nearly out of her mind with fear of Communists. It would be said that she hid in her room and displayed symptoms of advanced paranoia and was totally unable to carry on a conversation. But Rue's report indicates that she had a clear purpose in mind for the trip, that—for at least part of this time—she seemed relaxed and cheerful and displayed both a generally peaceful frame of mind and a positive outlook for the future.

111

There was an unsettling contradiction here—unfortunately, one difficult to reconcile, because this was the last personal interview she would ever give.

24

Pearl Harbor was attacked about the time *Badlands of Dakota* hit the theaters. The country was suddenly in the midst of a global war and it was the only topic of conversation in town. Everyone Frances knew was suddenly lining up to get into the army, or work in some war-related industry, or donate their time and energy in some other way to the one great cause. America was totally mobilizing itself to fight fascism, and everything else—including the making of Hollywood movies— suddenly seemed terribly irrelevant.

The advent of the war appeared to have a particularly strong effect on Frances, who had always been caught up in the drama of world events. Her brother Wes was already in the army, and her sister Edith was living in Honolulu at the time and had personally witnessed the bombing. Throughout the first half of 1942, while names like Bataan and Doolittle and Coral Sea were entering the national vocabulary, she followed the events closely. Sometime during this first six months of the war, she came up with the idea of organizing a group of big-name movie actors to tour the army bases and perform classic plays for servicemen. She made elaborate

113

plans and even made a brief announcement to the press, but it never came off. The film community had never really forgotten her caustic remarks made in New York interviews—it was still almost universally accepted around town that she was a Communist and a troublemaker—and no studio was about to let its stars have anything to do with her.

In later years, a great deal would be written and said to the effect that Frances was turning into a hopeless and crazy drunk during this period. This would seem a gross exaggeration, though it is obvious she was beginning to drink more than usual and she was developing some serious emotional problems. Certainly she was lonely. Her marriage had been finished now for years (the divorce became final in June of that year). Her few affairs after Odets—reputedly with Harold Clurman in New York and one or two others in Hollywood—had usually ended with bad feelings on both sides, and her abortion had left her with terrible guilt feelings. She was also exhausted from overwork (she was only twenty-seven years old and had appeared in eighteen films, three Broadway plays, thirty major radio shows, seven stock company productions, and countless personal appearances). And beyond all this, there is evidence of another problem: It was widely accepted among her friends (and Frances herself later admitted) that she was developing a problem with amphetamines.

The drug amphetamine had been synthesized in a laboratory in 1927. Its first recognized medical use was to reduce nasal congestion in colds, and in 1932 it was marketed under the trade name of Benzedrine. Shortly thereafter, it was discovered that the drug was useful as an appetite depressant and could be used as a kind of "diet pill." Frances was a big girl who was constantly worried about her weight, and sometime after the drug was first put on the market, a doctor recommended it to her. She was known to take it periodically for that purpose all during her Hollywood and Broadway years. In those days, it was sold without prescription and very little was known about its side effects—the strange rush of confidence, exhilaration, and talkativeness that typically accompanies it. (Not until the 1970s, in fact, was it discovered that taken in sufficient quantity it can recreate perfectly the delusions of schizophrenia.) It's not clear exactly what quantity she was taking but it is fairly certain that during most of 1942—probably without even knowing it—she was becoming dependent on the drug and it often caused her to behave erratically.

In this somewhat volatile condition, she replaced an ailing Maureen O'Hara on a picture called *Son of Fury* at 20th Century-Fox that June. A historical drama based on the novel *Benjamin Blake*, it was the most expensive film in which she had ever appeared and a far cry from the paltry budget of something like *Among the Living*. It turned out to be an almost perfect screen entertainment, with something going for it in every department—a good script by Phillip Dunne, solid direction by John Cromwell, splendid photography by Arthur Miller, and a fine cast that included Tyrone Power (as Blake), George Sanders, Elsa Lanchester, and John Carradine. Best of all was the fact

115

that the ingenue role was played by Gene Tierney and Frances was given a more substantial romantic character part, in which she turned in a mature and masterfully restrained performance.

Frances was so good in the part that it might have been the watershed of her career—leading to a whole series of such roles. But immediately after finishing her scenes in *Fury,* something happened that would irrevocably change her life. On the chilly, damp evening of October 19, 1942, she got into her car to drive to a party at the home of the actress Deanna Durbin. While passing through the town of Santa Monica on the Pacific Coast Highway, she was stopped by a motorcycle policeman for driving in a dimout zone with her lights on. Frances had never been particularly fond of the police and was characteristically impatient during the obligatory lecture. When the officer asked to see her license, she discovered she had left it in another purse. When she resisted his attempt to ticket her ("You bore me," she told him), he arrested her. Loudly protesting her innocence, she was hauled into court, charged with drunken driving, and, without a breath test or benefit of attorney, given the unusually severe sentence of 180 days in jail, suspended.

As a West Seattle high-school junior, Frances Farmer first received national attention by winning a magazine's student writing contest with a controversial essay entitled "God Dies."

After high school, she began working her way
through the University of Washington as an
usherette at Seattle's Paramount Theater. She
later said the job gave her a lifelong distaste
for the movies.

Author's collection

Author's collection

Above: Frances as a freshman journalism student in 1931, selling subscriptions to the college humor magazine. After her first year of college, she switched her major to drama. Below, she appears at lower right, rehearsing for a university play. Left: a publicity picture for the university production of *Alien Corn,* a play which made her star of the drama department.

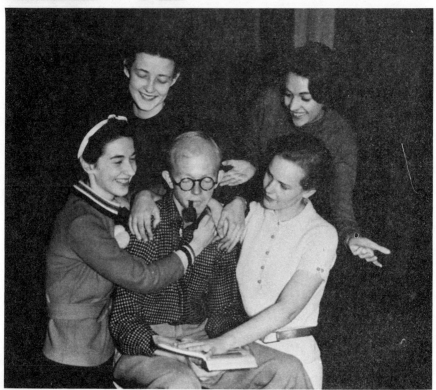

OIL FIRMS REPORT 'GAS' SUPPLY GONE

Il Draw on Pooled Seattle Reserves Today; Famine Only Twelve Days Distant

ger Companies Announce Flatly Nonunion Crews Will Move Tankers at Once

With a gasoline famine eatened in Seattle, repre-tatives of the large oil npanies announced flatly t night they would begin at e to move their strike-und fleet of tankers with union crews.

he menace of a gasoline short-with paralysis of all motor sportation was revealed in the ouncemnt of two of the largest companies that their supply was austed.

eginning this morning, one com-y will start drawing on the led reserves of the other com-ies and printed signs on the ops of their stations will inform motoring public that owing to ke conditions, the gasoline they ive may be "different than it a on the pump."

he other will beginning tapping pool tomorrow, it was asserted.

AY SUPPLY

fficials estimated that the gaso-, at its present rate of con-ption will last about twelve s with the fuel and diesel oil ation becoming so acute that companies were on a ration s for industry last night.

t the same time the business of Seattle took official cogniz-of the strike menace to the mercial life of the city when of them met at the Seattle mber of Commerce to hear the rt of Daniel W. Hone of San cisco, legal representative of oleum industry.

one told the business men that whole issue involved in the e is the closed shop.

SED SHOP ISSUE

We have granted the wage in-ases demanded and have im-ved working conditions," he

---

A Seattle Mother's

WARNING AGAINST RED TEACHERS

Parent Unable to Halt Girl's Trip to Russia

'SCHOOL INFLUENCED'

"If I must sacrifice my daughter to Communism I hope other mothers save their daughters before they are turned into radicals in our schools."

In these words, **Mrs. Lillian V. Farmer** last night despaired of preventing her twenty-one-year-old daughter, Frances, University of Washington drama student, from visiting Soviet Russia at the expense of the Voice of Action, local radical newspaper.

Since Miss Farmer won the trip in a subscription contest staged by the publication, her mother has been making every effort to keep the girl from accepting the "prize" and visiting Russia—even going so far as appealing to the prosecutor's office to halt the visit. No solution was given her there.

GIRL DETERMINED

But her daughter declared last night that she is determined to go and will leave Saturday for New York by bus to board a steamer for Soviet Russia.

Meanwhile, a reservation for a banquet tomorrow night at the Y. M. C. A., at which Miss Farmer was to be formally awarded the prize, was canceled by Wesley Rennie, general secretary, upon learning the radical nature of the meeting.

"I'm afraid Frances may never return if she goes there," Mrs. Farmer said, "and even if she does she will be so swayed by Soviet propaganda that she will become a firm Communist.

"I telephoned them to strike Frances' name from the contest, but they refused."

Miss Farmer, however, declared she had no interest in Communism, has never been approached on the subject by anyone and is only interested in visiting Russia and other European countries to study drama—in which she intends to make a career.

"I'm sorry mother is objecting to the trip," Miss Farmer said. "But it is a splendid chance to further my dramatic career and I'm not going to turn it down unless some unforeseen circumstance arises."

Mrs. Farmer said she was as-

FRANCES FARMER
Mother's Pleas in Vain

her daughter was thrown in contact with at the university.

"The university and high schools are hotbeds of Communism," she asserted. "In the contest Frances and those supporting her had a list of university and high school teachers who were interested in the labor movement. They helped her get subscriptions to the paper.

"Something should be done immediately to clean the schools of radical teachers before they sway other girls and boys away from American ideals."

Miss Farmer denied that members of either the University or high school faculties gave her any

---

LONDON DROPS HOPE OF NAZI COOPERATION

Hitler Demands at Berlin Talks Believed to Have Shattered Idea of General Conference

By WILLIAM HILLMAN
(Copyright, 1935, by Universal Service.)

LONDON, March 28. — Prospect of European cooperation with Germany in a system of "collective security" has been shattered as a result of the Berlin talks between Chancellor Hitler and British Foreign Secretary Simon, it was authoritatively stated tonight.

Hope of holding a general "peace" conference in which Germany, as well as the other European powers, would partake to bring about general settlements, has been virtually abandoned.

Europe is now definitely faced with the problem of building up old-time alliances unless Hitler modifies his present attitude.

This is the opinion expressed to Universal Service in higher London circles tonight.

SIMON SEES KING

Today Sir John Simon went to Buckingham Palace to report the Berlin conversations to King George. Subsequently he told the house of commons that his talks with Hitler had disclosed considerable divergence of opinion between Britain and Germany.

Such a change is not expected, in view of Hitler's blunt, if polite, review of Germany's position. Hitler, I am able to reveal, told Simon that Germany will return to the League of Nations only on three conditions. The conditions are:

1 —Equality of status for Germany.

2 —Change of the league covenant.

3 —Return to Germany of her former colonial empire.

Hitler told Simon that, with the restoration of her former colonies, Germany would be prepared to help Britain police the British empire routes against Bolshevism and the "colored" menace.

CITES JAPAN

The Fuehrer declared he could not agree to return to the league without the colonies while Japan was permitted to retain former German possessions, although she is not a member of the league.

Germany's attitude in this respect reveals the fundamental difference between Britain and Germany which Simon had in mind today when he declared there was "con-

---

(right edge column — partial text)

H SI B'

Cit F

B with nett perl larg and Burg pros Judg yest B ing Nav man exec base von ices tion coll

F Mar von clie serv form a m tua Nav the Elvi coll only

'OPI In ray' his cont mad and defr tech

In ever that Mur the city cials men true

INT B ray nan ing i pres out suite Bur

In March, 1935, Frances won a contest sponsored by Seattle's Communist newspaper, *The Voice of Action*—and a first prize VIP tour of the Soviet Union. The controversy over this trip turned into one of the most heated episodes in the history of Northwest radicalism.

Frances at age twenty, leaving for the Soviet
Union aboard the *Manhattan*. Despite her
denials, the Russians regarded her as the
official representative of America's Communist
youth.

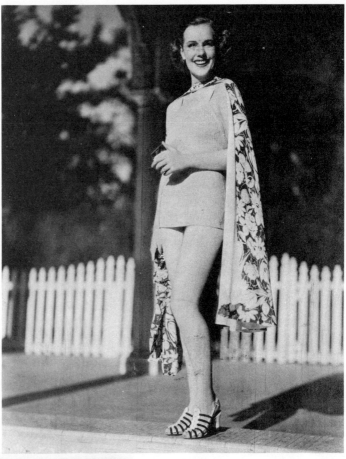

Within weeks of returning from Russia, Frances was given a screen test and a long-term contract with Paramount Studios. Shown above in an early publicity shot. Left, Frances had been in Hollywood only a few months when she became a hit in *Rhythm on the Range*. Bing Crosby starred.

Below, with her parents, Ernest and Lillian Farmer, on the set of *Rhythm on the Range* in 1936. At left, the film version of Edna Ferber's *Come and Get It* made her a major star at the age of twenty-one.

With Edward Arnold and Jack Oakie in RKO's *Toast of New York* in 1937. Cary Grant co-starred. At right, in *Escape from Yesterday*, 1938.

Above: with her first
husband, actor Leif
Erickson, and her mother,
just before leaving
Hollywood to join New
York's Group Theater for
Golden Boy. At right,
Frances and Leif,
vacationing in Seattle
shortly before their
separation.

Seattle *Post-Intelligencer*

With her parents in Seattle, soon after filming *Badlands of Dakota* in 1940. This was her last public interview before her arrest and a decade of troubles with police and psychiatrists.

Seattle *Post-Intelligencer*

In 1942, she co-starred with Tyrone Power in
Son of Fury, a role which promised to revitalize
her career.

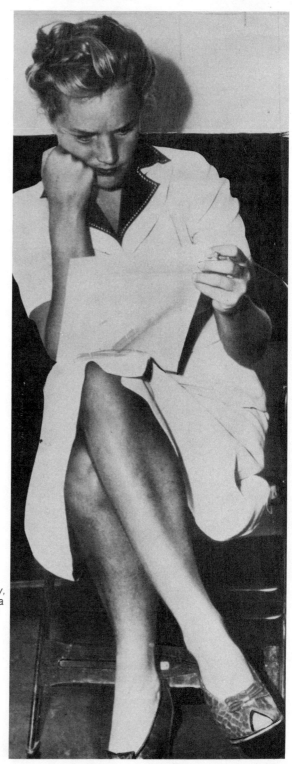

Shortly after finishing *Fury*, Frances was arrested for a minor traffic violation and sentenced to 180 days in jail, suspended. Shown here after booking at police station, October, 1942.

In January, 1943, she was arrested in her hotel room and dragged to Santa Monica police court and charged with failure to report to her parole officer.

Denied use of the phone after sentence was passed, she got into a physical and verbal brawl with matrons, officers, and reporters and was hauled off to jail to serve her sentence.

Above, Lillian Farmer leaving for California after the courtroom incident, January, 1943. Frances was confined to a private mental institution and given massive doses of insulin shock. Some months later, her mother committed her to Western State Hospital at Steilacoom, Washington. Judge John A. Frater, shown third from right with Boy Scouts, was the influential political figure in charge of the mysterious legal proceedings.

Frances reading fan mail after release from her
first round of treatment at Steilacoom, July,
1944.

Placed under her mother's
guardianship, Frances
made several escape
attempts. In July, 1944, she
again made headlines
when arrested for
vagrancy in Antioch,
California. Shown at right
and below in police
custody at Antioch.

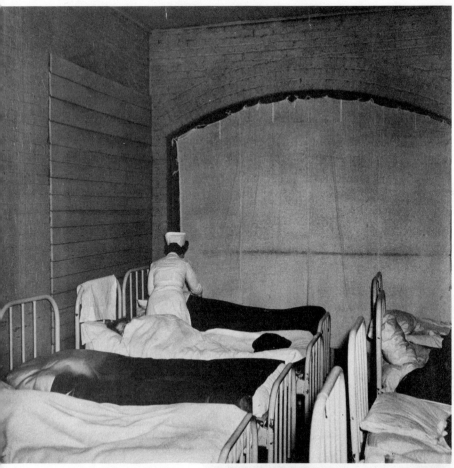

At right, Lillian Farmer shows reporters how she helped identify Frances from the Antioch photographs. In May, 1945, Lillian inexplicably committed Frances to Steilacoom again, where she remained for the next five years—most of that time in the violent ward under appallingly primitive conditions. Above, a typical Steilacoom ward in the 1940s.

Seattle *Post-Intelligencer*

Lillian Farmer, posing for a photograper
during her last interview in October, 1947. She
blamed her daughter's tragedy on "World
Communism."

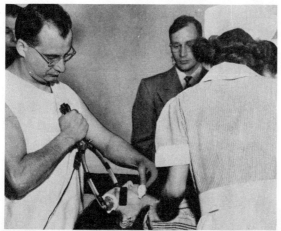

Top: Electroshock administered at Steilacoom. Frances was subjected to hundreds of such treatments yet remained defiant of hospital authorities. Her case attracted some of the nation's leading psychiatrists to Steilacoom—including Dr. Walter Freeman, the dean of American lobotomy, shown at bottom left explaining his theories on an early television broadcast.

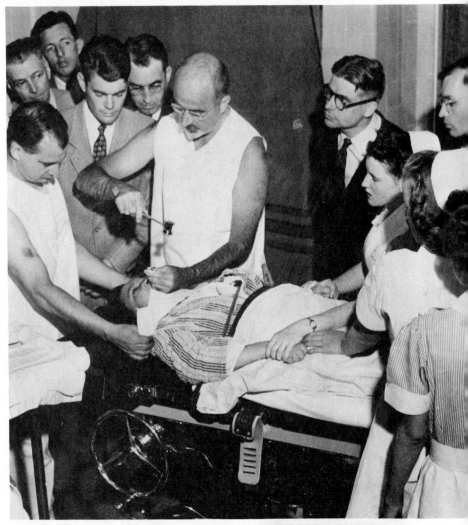

Dr. Freeman performing transorbital lobotomy experiments at Steilacoom in 1948. After her release from Steilacoom, Frances left Seattle and lived for several years under her married name in Eureka, California. In 1957, reporters found her working as a clerk (at right) in the Sheraton-Palace Hotel in San Francisco.

Below: Hugh O'Brien and Martha Hyer welcome Frances back to Hollywood in 1957 in an unsuccessful comeback attempt. At left, the Las Vegas wedding of Frances and Lee Mikesell in 1958.

With Bobby Driscoll on the set of her last
movie, *The Party Crashers*, a 1958 teenage
exploitation picture.

25

When a major star was arrested for drunk-
enness in the '40s, particularly a female star,
it was a serious scandal which could jeopardize an
entire career. In Frances' case it was worse, both
because she was already so controversial and
because she steadfastly refused to admit she had
been drinking heavily on the night in question (her
claim was that she had had exactly three beers earlier in the evening). Accordingly, the Hollywood
community completely ostracized her. She was
excluded from dinner parties. Her name vanished
from the columns. A studio could no longer get in-
surance for a picture in which she had a starring
role. The situation was so alarming that her agent
called and frankly advised her to get out of town for
as long as it took for this thing to blow over.

A few weeks before her arrest, she had met a
producer at a rally for the benefit of migratory Mexican workers who had offered her the lead in an up-
coming picture. It was an independent, low-budget
production shooting in Mexico called *Hostages*, a
semi-left-wing avant-garde endeavor whose pro-
ceeds would go partly to help indigent Mexican
workers. She had originally refused the offer but

141

now she hastily reconsidered. She knew almost nothing about it, but it seemed an ideal opportunity to get out of town and keep working at the same time. Still hurt, upset, and very nervous, and not thinking at all clearly, she called the man back and accepted the part without even seeing the script.

When she got to Mexico City, she quickly realized that she had made a mistake. The movie turned out to be a hopelessly amateur production which was being almost totally improvised. At the same time, back in the States *Son of Fury* promised to be highly successful, and she suddenly didn't want to damage her career further by associating her name with this pathetic venture. She moved into a small, ratty hotel on the outskirts of Mexico City where the company was staying and tried to figure out how she was going to extricate herself. It is not clear exactly what happened next—there is one confused account that Frances was beaten up by a member of the crew, but it is doubtful—and the only thing known for certain is that within several days she became desperately ill.

Stories of this illness were cabled back to Hollywood and triggered a wild blast of rumors. Louella Parsons reported in her column that Frances had had a nervous breakdown and had been forced by the American Embassy to go to a sanitarium. Interational News Service reported:

> Frances Farmer, widely known Hollywood actress, is seriously ill in a Mexico City sanitarium, columnist Louella O. Parsons reported yesterday.

142

Miss Farmer is so very sick, according to Miss Parsons, that the American Embassy has sent her to the hospital.

Informed of the report, the mother of the actress, Mrs. Lillian Farmer, expressed surprise and disbelief.

"I know that Frances was in no condition to work when she went to Mexico City," she explained, "but I am positive she had not been taken to a hospital. I talked with her long distance last week, and she was feeling fine and hoped to come home for Christmas. Surely I would have been notified if she had a breakdown!"

I flew to Mexico City to see what I could find out about this mysterious "breakdown." There was a partial account of the incident in the files of the American Embassy there and a full rundown in several English-language newspapers. What had actually happened was that Frances had simply come down with a terrible case of *turista,* the dysenterylike illness which has been afflicting foreigners in Mexico since the days of Cortés. She had become so sick that the Embassy *had* been called in, but rather than sending her to a hospital, someone on the ambassador's staff decided that—since she was a controversial public figure filming a questionable movie—the wisest thing to do was to get her out of the country as soon as possible. A detachment of Mexican police came and drove her for several days all the way to the Laredo, Texas, border sta-

143

tion, where she was unceremoniously deposited. She stayed in a small hotel there until she had sufficiently recovered and then cabled her brother for money to get back to Hollywood.

While I was in Mexico City, I looked around for traces of the unfinished film *Hostages*. I wandered around for several days talking to veterans of the Mexican film industry (with no success) and then decided to go back to Hollywood and pick up the trail again. Just as I was leaving, I came down with a particularly virulent case of the same disease that had immobilized Frances. I lay in bed for days, unable to move, except to crawl to the bathroom. I have never felt so awful, and the only thing I could think of was how horrible it must have been for poor Frances, having to drive for days in a bumpy car across the worst part of Mexico in this condition. She must have truly wanted to die.

To make matters worse, the story—which spread all over Hollywood before she got back—somehow came out that she had been deported from Mexico for "undesirable behavior." A major star had been arrested for drunken driving and now had been deported from Mexico! ("Mexico, for crissakes," one Paramount executive claimed, "nobody gets deported from Mexico.") The whole experience was a disaster for her. It added immeasurably to the animosity toward her in Hollywood, and for the first time raised the specter of mental illness (based on no greater authority than Louella Parsons speculating on a rumor), and set her up for the extraordinary chain of events that would take place over the next few months.

26

When I got back from Mexico, I drove out to the Burbank Studios to do a story on the filming of *All the President's Men*. It was the same sound stage where Frances had shot scenes for *Flowing Gold* all those years before, and it looked uncannily like the city room of the *Washington Post*. The director, Alan Pakula, told me that his film was a reflection of the paranoia of our time, a monument to the all-prevailing cultural theme of the '70s, which is that "if you dig deep enough into any mystery, you'll find some kind of evil conspiracy." I wandered around the set watching Redford and Hoffman look glamorous and was suddenly filled with doubts. Was I somehow morbidly caught up in all this? Was I trying too hard to find some mysteries of Frances Farmer that didn't really exist? At this point I really did not know.

I went back to Hollywood, armed with news clippings, police reports, and the hazy recollections of eyewitnesses, and spent several days tracing the events after the disastrous trip to Mexico. Earlier that same day, I had spoken to Dalton Trumbo, the famous scriptwriter and Hollywood radical, who knew Frances during this period. He said: "You have to realize that they were out to get Frances and she knew it. Who? The cops. Why? The political thing. The migrant worker thing. You name it. They wanted to bust that kid wide open and they finally had the opportunity."

When Frances got back to Hollywood, she discovered that—to save money while she was away—her business manager had sublet the Malibu house and moved all her possessions into a room at the Knickerbocker Hotel. She also discovered that she was the focus of a veritable tidal wave of gossip that was not about to subside. Her friends advised her that, if she didn't come out of hiding and face down the rumors, she might never work again.

Frances' natural inclination was to get away when things got rough, to hide and lose herself in her poetry. She was by nature a compulsively private person, and she hated night life and gossip and the entire Hollywood scene. But this thing was not about to blow over and she soon realized that she was fighting for her life as an actress. From her new base of operations at the Knickerbocker Hotel, she threw herself into the task. She called Louella and tried to explain what had happened in Mexico. She accepted the first movie role that came along (a part in a low-budget Monogram melodrama called *No Escape*). She forced herself to go out and mix in public, and to bolster her sagging energy she consumed an enormous quantity of amphetamine.

By the morning of January 13, 1943, she was already in an explosively nervous state. She went to the studio but was so tense and nervous she was unable to shoot her scenes. While she was trying to collect herself on the set, she somehow got into an argument with a studio hairdresser named Edna Burge (Burge cannot remember what the argument was about), and in the course of a shouting match, Frances slapped the woman, knocking her down and dislocating her jaw. After this incident, Frances left the studio and drove back to the Knickerbocker Hotel. Some hours later, she went to the hotel bar and had several drinks with a group of friends. The group eventually got drunk and quite rowdy and an argument broke out—apparently not including Frances. The manager expelled them from the bar and Frances then went upstairs to her room and tried to get some sleep.

In the meantime, Edna Burge had become so angry that she pressed charges for assault. When she went to the police, they said there was already a warrant out for Frances Farmer's arrest because she had not paid the remaining half of the $250 fine for her drunk driving arrest. A detachment of police was immediately sent to the Knickerbocker Hotel. Detective Earl Rienbold pounded on her door. When she didn't answer at once—Frances usually slept in the nude—the officers opened the door with a passkey. As she saw the room flooding with police, she tried to run from them. They pursued her (according to one account, breaking down the bathroom door to get to her), restrained her, forced her to get dressed, and carried her off to the Santa Monica jail. With a grin, Detective Rienbold told reporters at the jail that the actress swore at them, using words he had never heard come from a lady's mouth, and ran around before them "less than scantily clad."

The story of the arrest was heavily covered by the Los Angeles and Hollywood press and ran in newspapers all over the country. The barroom argument and the Burge slapping episode were inflated to such an extent that it sounded as if she had been on a maniacal twenty-four-hour spree. Several papers actually erroneously reported that she had taken off her clothes and paraded down Sunset Strip. (On hearing the news, Mrs. Lillian Farmer told the Seattle press that it might be a "publicity stunt" designed to give her the true-to-life experience of a jail inmate. "They might be planning a picture for her with jail scenes in it and want her to gave a performance based on actual experience. If it isn't a publicity stunt, then this is Frances' first serious trouble. She was a model child.")

But the most widely publicized portion of the entire incident was the fact that Frances used four-letter words. The arresting officers were quoted over and over again that their "ears were burning" from the language she used. The UP reported that at police headquarters she listed her occupation as such an unorthodox one (presumably "cocksucker") that "it caused the police booking officer to jump when he read it." This fact would warrant an entire side story to itself in many editions. The whole thrust of the publicity was that a foulmouthed, left-wing movie star had caused a lot of trouble and had gotten just what she deserved.

148

27

The next morning, after half a night in jail, Frances Farmer was marched into police-court Judge Marshall Hickson's courtroom. Her eyes were bloodshot, her blond hair straggling, her blue suit torn and mussed. She had not slept for some thirty-six hours. She was mentally groggy and visibly nervous and angrily indignant at what was happening to her. The court transcript reflected her frayed nerves.

> JUDGE HICKSON: Since you appeared in this court on October 24, have you had anything to drink?
>
> F.F.: Yes, I drank everything I could get, including Benzedrine.
>
> JUDGE HICKSON: You were advised that if you took one drink of liquor or failed to be a law-abiding citizen ..."
>
> F.F. (interrupting): What do you expect me to do? I get liquor in my orange juice—in my coffee. Must I starve to death to obey your laws?
>
> JUDGE HICKSON: Is it true that you were in a fight at a Hollywood nightclub?

149

F.F.: Yes, I was fighting for my country and myself.

JUDGE HICKSON: Have you driven a car since you were placed on probation?

F.F.: No, I haven't, but only because I couldn't get my hands on one.

JUDGE HICKSON: Have you reported to your probation officer as directed?

F.F.: No, I never saw him. Why didn't he show up?

JUDGE HICKSON (incredulously): Did you expect him to look you up?!

F.F.: I expected him to be around so I could get a look at his face.

Several of the spectators were giggling now. Judge Hickson was turning red. He was not about to be mocked by this arrogant and sarcastic movie star. He pounded his gavel and sentenced her to serve the 180 days in jail.

As the judge was leaving the bench, Frances shouted at him: "I haven't any lawyer!"

The judge kept on walking.

"What I want to know is do I have any civil rights?!"

The judge continued walking.

Frances walked quietly to the rear of the courtroom and asked to use the phone to call a lawyer. When the matron refused, Frances ran for the phone. Two officers grabbed for her. She fought back. One officer was floored and the matron and another officer bruised as they carried her out of the courtroom screaming something about a "broken heart" and her "civil rights."

She was taken to the Los Angeles county jail to begin serving her sentence and the scene there was even uglier. Crowds of reporters and photographers mobbed around the desk while a struggling and kicking Frances, confined now in a straitjacket, was booked.

She screamed at the reporters ("Rats! Rats! Rats!") and traded insults with police captain Charles Fitzgerald, who had come over for the occasion."Why can't you be a nice girl?" he smiled and taunted her.

"Who wrote your script?" Frances snapped back. "And why in hell don't you do something about that potbelly?"

"I got that from eating, sister, not drinking."

The booking sergeant asked for her occupation.

"I'm an actress—you know that. Just put me down as a vag ... vagrant vagabond."

When she was finally turned over to the jail matron, she appeared almost relieved. "The judge sentenced me to 180 days," she said. "Where do I eat? Where do I sleep? Where do I brush my teeth?"

151

28

It was painful to read that transcript. She *did* sound irrational, and yet it was also exactly how anyone who knew Frances might have expected her to act under the circumstances. The crack about getting liquor in her food (which ran as a headline in many papers) was an almost direct quote from her nutritional-minded mother. Frances was always sarcastic and rebellious toward what she considered misused authority, and of course her impulse was not to sound calm and judicious but rather to demand her civil rights. She had been awake for over a day and a half, pulled from bed in the dead of night, and roughed up by a squad of gestapo-like police. And through it all she consistently demanded and seems to have been denied a lawyer.

What happened next is not apparent from the record. All it says is that instead of being sent to jail to serve her sentence, Frances was placed in a private sanitarium. Weeks of research through official files provided no explanation. No one in City Hall or the various courts involved knew anything about her. ("Is she the one who wrote the cookbook?") There was also almost no mention of any of these events in the autobiography. Yet a full account was blazoned across the front page of a thirty-three-year-old issue of the *Los Angeles Times*.

The morning after the courtroom melee, an Alhambra psychiatrist named Thomas H. Leonard read the newspaper accounts and decided that Frances Farmer was mentally ill. It is still a mystery as to exactly how or why Dr. Leonard got involved in the case. He appears to have had no connection whatsoever with Frances or the Farmer family. Rather he had followed her career (and, presumably, Louella Parsons' column) and took it upon himself to enter the case as an "interested party." As any psychiatrist could do under California law, he simply went to the Superior Court and filed a complaint requesting that he be permitted to examine Frances to determine her sanity.

The Superior Court acted swiftly on the complaint and she was removed from jail and brought before Dr. Leonard that same day. He found her, he later reported to the court, "hostile and uncooperative." She refused to recognize his authority and was extremely sarcastic ("Well, where are the instruments? When are you going to start the torture? I thought you would brand me with a hot iron.") Leonard later told Judge Dudley S. Valentine that he asked her a question and she responded by saying: "That question is insulting, irrelevant, and impudent. Besides, it's none of your——— business." Dr. Leonard also told the judge that she told him she had not been able to sleep in jail because the lights were left on and she had heard "voices" all night that bothered her. All this led the

153

doctor to quickly diagnose her condition as "manic-depressive psychosis." He recommended that she be ordered to an appropriate mental health facility for "treatment."

The court transferred Frances to the psychiatric ward of the Los Angeles General Hospital on Wednesday, January 20, 1943. A hearing was ordered and her parents flew down from Seattle to attend. (Frances seemed overjoyed to see them and apologized over and over again for the "terrible embarrassment" she must have caused them.) In the course of the hearing, the doctors and her parents discussed the various aspects of her unorthodox lifestyle—her leftist political affiliations, her numerous solitary retreats, her alleged breakdown in Mexico, and her strange outburst in police court—and, put together, they seemed to create a very strange behavior pattern. Mrs. Farmer defended her daughter by testifying: "A layman can't understand an emotional, high-strung person like Frances. I think I know more about her than any other person in the world. Frances is unbalanced from her past year's experiences of frustration in her career." After Dr. Leonard's findings were read, the Farmers agreed that Frances probably needed treatment and would be better off in a "rest home" for at least six months. They did not, however, feel that a legal commitment hearing was in order, as the doctors strongly recommended.

The big surprise that came out of the hearing—and by far the most compelling argument against her—seemed to be the fact that Frances had no money. Since 1936, she had earned over one million

154

dollars, after taxes (according to the figures documented in her lawsuit with Traube). She had made no investments and purchased no property. She had never so much as bought a new car. Her business agents testified that she had "squandered" all her money—given it away to Communists, migrant workers, Spanish Civil War groups, her own family—and was now completely destitute. The only private facility available to an actress in this financial situation was the screen actors' sanitarium at La Crescenta in the San Fernando Valley, where the Motion Picture Relief Fund could arrange for her free admission.

She stayed in the General Hospital psychiatric ward again that night, resting comfortably. Two nurses who were on duty that evening remember that Frances seemed appalled by the strange scene around her and the numb, lifeless faces that made up the P ward, but not particularly frightened or concerned about her own safety. One nurse recalls that Frances saw a haggard woman weeping in the corner of the ward and she went over and tried to comfort her, even singing a song from one of her movies to calm the woman. It was obvious from her attitude that Frances seemed to think her predicament was all a ghastly mistake, just one more public hassle that would be cleared up in the morning.

29

While Frances spent yet another night inside
the hospital, outside the whole affair was
receiving more publicity than any Hollywood event
since the death of Carole Lombard. Pictures of
Frances battling the police made the cover of several magazines and the front page of practically every
newspaper in the country. Press accounts were almost callously unsympathetic and seemed to gloat
over Dr. Leonard's statements ("Frances is a very
sick girl"), which ran unqualified. The headlines
were particularly cruel: FRANCES FARMER PLACED
IN PSYCHOPATHIC WARD, MOVIE STAR IS MENTALLY
ILL and even simply FRANCES FARMER INSANE.

Despite such damning press coverage many
people at the time seemed to believe she was being
railroaded because of her politics and her unconventional life-style. Over three hundred theatrical people in New York, including Claire Luce, John Gold-
en, and her former agent Shepard Traube, signed a
petition and telegraphed it to the judge:

> We the undersigned are shocked at the harsh
> decision in regard to Miss Frances Farmer.
> However unfortunate recent events have

156

been, she is a gifted artist and should be afforded sympathetic treatment. . . .

The columnist John Rosenfield backhandedly defended her in a long editorial column:

> The Frances Farmer incident should never have happened. This unusually gifted actress was no threat against law and order or the public safety. Something that began as merely a traffic reprimand grew into a case of personal violence, a serious traffic charge and a jail sentence. And all because a sensitive high-strung girl was on the verge of a nervous breakdown. . . . Miss Farmer, who is no prodigy of emotional stability or sound business management, needed a lawyer one unhappy night last winter. A helping hand might have extradited her immediately from nothing more than a traffic violation. The terrible truth is that she stood alone, and lost.

Tyrone Power and other friends tried to get in and see her, but by this time she had already been taken to the sanitarium at La Crescenta.

When Frances entered the sanitarium, it was as if she had been swallowed up. As far as the records in Los Angeles were concerned, there was simply no further mention of her. I drove out to La Cresenta, just north of Glendale, and the sanitarium was still there, a very small, very quiet private hospital then on the very outskirts of Los Angeles. No one there remembered anything at all about Frances Farmer. It was years ago and she had not been there very long. But there was a smattering of old records around and they tell a story surprisingly similar to one Frances would give journalist Edward Keyes in a true-confession article many years later.

At first she welcomed the apparent peacefulness of the place and the reduced pace of her life. She was given a cheerful enough room. The nurses seemed considerate and sympathetic. She played Ping-Pong and caught up on her reading and took long contemplative strolls around the grassy hospital grounds. ("She seems fully recovered and is now the same Frances Farmer you knew when she first came to Hollywood," one psychiatrist there told a reporter.) After several months of this forced creative inactivity, however, she became restless and depressed. She got into arguments with the nurses. She didn't want to see visitors. Most of all, she wanted out of there and back into some constructive form of work.

The psychiatrists of La Crescenta were alarmed at this change in Frances' behavior. Within a week they had come to the conclusion that some sort of radical therapy was needed to "calm her down." They wrote Lillian Farmer in Seattle and asked for permission to use electroshock treatments. When Mrs. Farmer balked at the use of such drastic measures and refused, they wrote back and suggested insulin shock treatments. They told her it was quite harmless and would be extremely effective in treating the symptoms of depression that Frances had been displaying. On May 15, 1943, Lillian Farmer granted permission and Frances' medical history file was placed in a bright red folder.

158

30

Insulin shock was a relatively new therapy which had been devised by the eminent psychiatrist Manfred Sakel in Vienna less than ten years before. The idea behind it was to induce convulsions and stun the mental patient's sensibilities with a massive shock caused by injecting insulin into the system, after which the mental "pieces" would fall back into a more realistic (or euphoric) pattern. Later this treatment was found to be both dangerous and inefficient—as well as causing many unpleasant and unpredictable side effects—and it was replaced with other forms of shock. But in 1943 it was accepted psychiatric procedure for dealing with any kind of mild depression and Frances was immediately put on an intensive ninety-day program.

One morning she was taken into a small white room in the rear of the sanitarium and told to lie down on a cot. A doctor came in and said they were giving her something to "isolate her tensions." He kneeled down and injected her arm with a hypodermic syringe filled with insulin. The walls and ceiling suddenly closed in on her and she passed out. When she regained consciousness, her body was trembling and drenched with perspiration. She felt, she told the doctor, "indescribably humiliated." She ob-

159

jected so strenously that the dosage was increased. For the next few months, she was wheeled into that same white room two or three times a week and jabbed into shock.

Frances reacted very badly to the insulin shock treatments. She became terribly upset and genuinely frightened by what they were doing to her. She claimed she was losing her ability to recall even the simplest things. When she tried to read, she was unable to concentrate on the lines. When she tried to write poetry, it no longer came. She had gone to the sanitarium voluntarily, she said, because she realized she needed a rest, but the sanitarium was systematically destroying the only thing she had ever been able to hold onto in life—her faith in her artistic creativity.

The records report that Frances became so upset over the insulin injections that she tried to escape. One day in the early fall of 1943, she was strolling through the sanitarium grounds, as she was permitted to do each day before lunch. While the guard was looking the other way, she ran to the back wall and made a dash for it. Before they caught up with her, she hitchhiked to her half sister Rita's house in Venice and called her mother. When Mrs. Farmer found out about the ill effects of the insulin treatments, she angrily came down and tried to get Frances released.

The doctors of La Crescenta did not like the idea of having a patient taken away from them in the middle of treatment and they did everything they could to prevent it. Since Frances had not been declared legally insane, however, there was little

160

they could do (in fact, given her status, the insulin shock treatments had probably been administered illegally), and when her mother had a lawyer put up $500 bond, she was promptly released. Still, these doctors would go to court and initiate extradition proceedings against Frances, and for the next year there would be a bitter struggle to have her returned.

31

Lillian Farmer accompanied Frances back to Seattle by train on September 14, 1943. They were greeted at the King Street Station by E. M. Farmer, who kissed Frances tearfully and then helped her into the car. She looked, according to the one reporter there to cover the homecoming, "pale . . . gaunt and weak . . . obviously distraught." She seemed angry and terrified and terribly confused at the incredible things that were happening to her. She was also still suffering the aftereffects of almost unthinkably massive insulin shock (which classically include nervousness, loss of memory, and a frustrating inability to concentrate), and would continue to suffer them for many months to come.

During the unusually bleak winter of 1943–44, Frances stayed in Seattle trying to pull herself together. Numerous old friends dropped by to see her and they recall that she seemed to be making a concentrated effort to sort out all the extraordinary things that had happened to her during the past ten years. The more she thought about it, the more she became convinced she should take a long rest and forget her shattered film career. She had never really felt comfortable in the public spotlight, and the fame and money obviously meant nothing to her. By temperament, she always thought of herself as more of a writer than an actress anyway, and now more than ever she needed time to herself. On the strength of *Son of Fury*, her agent had put together another film offer for her later in the year, but Frances had firmly decided to turn it down and give up any connection with acting. One day she sat her mother down and told her this. It was, as it turned out, the wrong thing to say.

Lillian Farmer was by this time nearly seventy years old. She lived alone in the crumbling house in West Seattle, long separated from her husband and her numerous causes, and comforted only by the success of her children. The idea that Frances would *willingly* give up the great American dream of being a Hollywood star, would turn her back on fame and fortune, seemed to confirm everything the doctors of La Crescenta had told her. At first she tried to change Frances' mind. She worked on her day and night to convince her she was making a terrible mistake. She frantically called Paramount and other studios and tried to make movie deals for her. She made Frances—still suffering the aftereffects of insulin shock—so nervous and upset that she began to fight back verbally (something she had *never* done in her life), and soon bitter arguments were breaking out that all the neighbors could hear.

There are several conflicting versions of what happened next. The only thing that is certain is that Mrs. Farmer—in a remarkably short period of time—became convinced that Frances was behaving totally irrationally and needed to be institutionalized. She came to believe that their unusually tight mother-daughter relationship had been destroyed by years of Communist influence. She became obsessed with the idea that Frances had been driven insane by the Group Theater. It is also not clear whether Mrs. Farmer went to the authorities or the authorities came to her. But she had several mysterious meetings with various city officials that March and somehow became convinced that it was necessary to swear out a public complaint against her daughter.

On the morning of March 21, 1944, Frances came down to breakfast as usual. Mrs. Farmer was standing nervously in the foyer staring out the window. When Frances sat down at the breakfast table, her mother suddenly appeared excited. "Hurry and finish your juice," she said. "The boys are here."

"What boys?"

Frances looked up just in time to see three attendants come rushing through the back door. They grabbed her as she sat at the table, bloodied her face, wrestled her into a straitjacket, and dragged her kicking and screaming to the psychiatric ward of Seattle's public Harborview Hospital.

32

In the State of Washington, as in most parts of the country, a civil commitment proceeding could be initiated against an individual by any "interested party." On the surface it looked as if Lillian Farmer had simply gone to Superior Court and sworn out a complaint. The police had come and Frances had vanished into the judicial process. But still, the nagging questions remained: How could anyone as famous in Seattle as Frances Farmer be swept away so fast and so quietly? Who had Lillian Farmer approached or who had approached her? How was Frances permitted to defend herself?

I called the State Department of Social and Health Services. They told me that the commitment records for those years would fall under the King County Sanity Commission, which no longer existed. I was transferred to another clerk from the Department of Records. This clerk looked around for fifteen minutes and then told me the records for that particular case seemed to be missing, or more likely had been misplaced in moving years ago. One of my researchers thought there would have to be a duplicate copy of the complaint on file in the King County Court House. I went down to the Court

House and, sure enough, on file and untouched for over thirty years, was a complaint against Frances—filed under her married name, Mrs. F. E. Anderson.

The complaint said that Mrs. Farmer stated that Frances had rejected her profession and means of livelihood, had frequently run off to be alone, and had been driven into a dangerously hysterical condition by various traumatic experiences of the past few years. She further stated: "Frances made some progress at home and showed no evidence of violence until the last three weeks. On March 12, she turned the radio on loudly which I knew would annoy the neighbors. I asked her to turn it down and she became quite angry, grabbed my wrists and pushed me into a chair. My arms became black and blue. I realized at once that she needs institutional care, as I am entirely unable to control her at home."

It seems extraordinary but, under the law, the accusation of insanity was all that was necessary for Frances to be considered an "insane person" and therefore subject to arrest. Lillian Farmer had met with a Superior Court judge named John A. Frater, who had signed an order which stated:

> In the matter of Mrs. F. E. Anderson, an insane person:
>
> A complaint having been duly filed in this court charging the above named Mrs. F. E. Anderson with being an insane person and unsafe to be at large, and it appearing to the Court that this is a case which should be

under observation in the King County Hospital at Harborview.

It is now hereby ordered that said patient be and is hereby committed to the King County Hospital at Harborview for observation and treatment until the further order of the Court.

It is further ordered that the Clerk of the Court is hereby directed to issue a warrant for the arrest of the above named insane person.

Harborview is an immense brown stone building on a hill that towers over the harbor and downtown business district of Seattle like a big ugly castle. When Frances was placed under arrest, she was taken there and placed in a crowded padded cell in the rear of the building to await a commitment hearing. She would now have to face a panel composed of some of the leading citizens of Seattle, and, as the "above named insane person," the burden would be on her to prove to them that she was *not* insane.

33

I had been chasing the ghost of this enigmatic movie star for well over a year now. I had read her letters, talked to people who had known her, retraced the path of her career—utterly determined to solve the mystery of her strange life and commitment. But I seemed to have reached a dead end with the legal process that had committed her. No one in a position to know anything would talk about the case. There were apparently no records of the proceedings or medical recomendations on file anywhere. My only recourse at this point was to turn my attention to the man in charge of those proceedings—the Honorable Justice John A. Frater.

I went to the public library and discovered—first of all—that Frater was no ordinary political hack. He was, in fact, the very pillar of the Seattle establishment in the 1940s. His father had been a Superior Court justice before him and the leading figure in the legal history of the State of Washington. Described as a prim, scholarly man with an aristocratic bearing and a "sense of destiny," Frater was a deacon of the Congregationalist Church, a Mason, a leader of the state's Republican Party, a power in the American Legion, and a hard-core political conservative. He was also a tough and somewhat merciless jurist who had once gotten national attention for a proposal that the city of Seattle establish a public whipping post to punish certain kinds of social undesirables.

The fact that Frater was such a devout and powerful conservative political leader was intriguing, and I began to delve deeper into his past life and record. It seems that the man had a long history of busting radicals. In the teens, he had been counsel for the Union Pacific Railroad and had become hardened from years of fighting Wobblies in and out of court. He had been very much a part of the reaction that had resulted in the Everett and Centralia massacres. Charges had been made that he had used and cooperated with the FBI in illegally persecuting political radicals in the '20s. But most interesting of all was the fact that during the Red scare of the '30s, this man had been a member and probably a leader of the group known as the American Vigilantes of Washington.

It further seems that Frater had been passionately involved with the case of Frances Farmer since the early '30s (a connection which, while it might have prevented him from presiding over a criminal trial, did not particularly disqualify him from presiding over an infinitely more powerful sanity hearing). He is remembered as having denounced her in numerous speeches on numerous occasions over the years. As a Christian, he had been shocked when she won a national award for writing an atheistic essay as a child. As a patriot, he had been appalled when she was a controversial University of Washington student traveling to the Soviet Union under the auspices of the Communist Party. As a citizen of Seattle, he had been outraged when she had spit in their faces after the success of *Come and Get It* and become an outspoken film star who flaunted her membership in un-American organizations. She was, in short, an embarrassment to the city he loved and the prime symbol of everything he had fought all his life.

It is not known exactly what happened on the morning of March 24, 1944, as Judge Frater walked into his office in the King County Courthouse to set the machinery in motion that would seal the fate of Frances Farmer. He spent most of the morning calling—and being called by—various city leaders, discussing the case. It is not known whom he telephoned or what was said, but this would undoubtedly be one of the most famous commitments in American history, and it is likely a number of important political figures were consulted as to how to handle the case. After this, he selected a young man named Charles Stone to serve as guardian *ad litem,* the attorney charged with protecting the legal rights of a defendant in a commitment proceeding. Finally, he called his old friend and the Northwest's leading psychiatrist, Dr. Donald A. Nicholson, and asked him to serve as examining physician.

The proceeding was now ready to begin and it was by any measure an extraordinary set of circumstances. One of America's most outspoken left-wing symbols was in a padded cell about to be

170

judged by one of the country's most powerful right-wing vigilantes. Though she had no way of knowing it, Frances had fallen into the hands of a man who had been damning her all her life. The result was, perhaps, inevitable.

34

The discovery that Frances had been committed by a member of the American Vigilantes of Washington seemed to change everything in my mind. All this time I had been trying to trace the progression of her "madness" and it now seemed entirely possible that she had not been mad at all. It seemed that her breakdown and various nervous problems could have been used as a convenient excuse to put her away. But it still didn't make sense. Maybe psychiatry was used as a vicious political weapon in Russia, but how could such a thing happen in this country with all its Constitutional safeguards? Even if vigilantes did everything they could to get rid of Frances, how could they possibly convince the entire mental health establishment of the State of Washington to go along with them?

I began to look for the records of her commitment proceedings, and not long after, a rather curious thing happened. Down in the Los Angeles offices of a magazine called *Freedom*, which had reprinted my original article on Frances Farmer, a strange, tall man in an excited state had come in and warned the editor to "stay away" from the story. The man said he had followed the Farmer case from the earliest days. He said he had discovered unbelievable, dangerous things involving very powerful political figures and had suffered terrible consequences because of it. He seemed genuinely frightened and before he disappeared, he said one word several times. That word was *Zioncheck*.

The editor called me and at first I didn't think much about it—I had had dozens of crank calls over the months. But the man did seem to know a number of very interesting things. He knew, for instance, intimate details about Frances' life and career that he would have no way of knowing without a great deal of research. He also was able to tell the editor the names and something about the background of every single figure involved in her commitment. Furthermore, the word *Zioncheck* vaguely rang a bell.

It took me less than five minutes in the library to learn that Zioncheck was Marion Zioncheck, a United States Congressman in the '30s, and that his story was almost identical to Frances Farmer's. Zioncheck was also a native of West Seattle. He had also been a controversial University of Washington student who as student body president shocked the Seattle establishment by one headline-grabbing escapade after another. After graduation he rallied the unemployed labor of Skid Road and got himself elected to Congress, representing Seattle's First Congressional District. In the nation's capital, he soon became known as "the Wild Man of Washington," the most controversial Congressman of the '30s and a self-proclaimed troublemaker who did everything he could to antagonize the establishment.

173

("I am a radical!" he once proclaimed before the Seattle Women's City Club, who hissed at him in mass.) He attacked the American Legion, chided the American Vigilantes of Washington, praised the Soviet Union, and, in one dramatic moment in April, 1936, denounced J. Edgar Hoover on the floor of the House of Representatives.

Two months after the Hoover incident, Zioncheck was mysteriously taken to a Washington, D.C., mental hospital for observation. He was kept incommunicado for several weeks, during which time he was treated by some of the nation's leading psychiatrists. After several escape attempts, he was released in a condition not unlike Frances' state after her insulin treatments. He returned to Seattle in this, as the papers of the time called it, "erratic" state, and within a few weeks inexplicably committed suicide by jumping or, some alleged, by being pushed out of the fifth floor of the Seattle Arctic Building. He was succeeded by Warren G. Magnuson, who went on to the U.S. Senate and became one of the most powerful and influential Senators in the nation.

Over a period of weeks, this mystery man was tracked down, and (very reluctantly) he submitted to an interview. His name was Stewart O. Jacobson and he was, in his own way, a famous figure in Seattle cultural history—and a character right out of Dashiell Hammett. In the early '30s, he had been a bodyguard for Marion Zioncheck. After Zioncheck's demise, he became a rather well-known private detective around town. In 1939, he made national headlines when he was charged (and acquitted) in a sensational murder case. All through the late '30s and early '40s, he did various "delicate" jobs for Seattle politicians and he was very much in a position to know—by the admission of any number of veterans of that era—where many of the skeletons were buried.

Jacobson contends that the power structure of Seattle wanted to get rid of both Frances Farmer and Marion Zioncheck because they were national embarrassments to the city. He claims that he was hired by several politicians to keep track of her before she was put away and, because of what he knew, he eventually lost his license and was forced out of Seattle. He detailed an elaborate conspiracy by citizen vigilantes to "do in" all the leading radicals of the Northwest by having them declared legally insane. He went on for hours—implicating every major politician in Washington State—and it was so fantastic that there was no way I could accept all of it. There did indeed seem to be a connection between the cases of Frances Farmer and Marion Zioncheck, but such a grand conspiracy theory implied all sort of things that didn't make any sense at all. Specifically, *why* should institutional psychiatry in Seattle and California and Washington, D.C., cooperate in such a plot?

The answer to this question—if there was one—had to lie with the psychiatrist assigned by Judge Frater to Frances' case—a noted neurologist named Donald A. Nicholson.

175

35

I spent most of the next few weeks trying to learn everything I could about Dr. Nicholson. I drove out to the Highlands, the old and exclusive residential area north of Seattle where he had lived, and spoke to his surviving family. I interviewed a number of prominent Seattleites who had known and worked with him in various community affairs over the years. Then I gathered as many of his private papers as I could find—both on file in the public library and in private hands—and pored over them.

I learned that Nicholson was born on Prince Edward Island, Canada, in February, 1874. He attended the University of Minnesota Medical School, where he became fascinated with the hidden inner workings of the human mind. After a brief internship at the State Hospital for the Male Insane at St. Peter's, Minnesota, he came to the wilds of Washington State to set up a pioneering psychiatric practice in 1906. He quickly made a name for himself in the medical circles of Seattle and became the Northwest's leading psychiatrist. Between the years 1906 and 1948 (when he died), he served as president of the King County Medical Society, president

176

of the Washington State Medical Association, and president of the Washington Society for Mental Hygiene.

Nicholson's had been an exceptional and successful career, but looking over his papers, there seemed to be endless questionable aspects of his practice, beyond the fact that he had made a small fortune. In his time, he had personally committed thousands of people to Washington State insane asylums, many of whom were obvious psychotics; but others more plainly criminals, anarchists, Wobblies, and other social undesirables. Nicholson prided himself on being able to judge a man's sanity on the basis of three short questions, and he had once stated that any man who embraced Communism was at least "suspect." Even more bothersome were his numerous political connections. He had worked with the FBI and moved socially with judges and legislators, and seemed to be in every way a functioning member of the governing hierarchy of the state. But perhaps the most significant thing about Nicholson's career was the fact that, in 1930, he had been the Washington delegate to the International Congress on Mental Hygiene.

This medical conference, which in recent years has become a controversial historical event, was, in effect, the first great gathering of the world's psychiatrists, convened for the purpose of creating an organization to "determine and further the goals" of the fledgling discipline of psychiatry. It was held in Washington, D.C., in May of 1930, and President Herbert Hoover was on hand to welcome some four thousand psychiatrists from fifty-three different

177

countries. Nicholson's notes state that it was "one of the most important milestones in the history of psychiatry," the first opportunity "since the founding of the mental hygiene movement to bring together mental hygiene workers from all parts of the world to discuss common problems, to exchange information and experience, and to lay plans for a concerted effort to advance the movement in all countries."

Working in small committees and seminars, the doctors at the conference came to the consensus that they had a very special kind of responsibility in the twentieth century. They alone had the knowledge that was required to "understand and control human behavior" and therefore they would have to organize themselves and assume a new kind of authority in modern society. The doctor who drafted the charter stated it succinctly: "Psychiatrists alone possess the superior intelligence and knowhow with which to alter materially and permanently human behavior. . . . Psychiatry must now decide what is to be the immediate future of the human race; no one else can. This is the prime responsibility of psychiatry. . . ."

It sounds incredible today but these doctors quite openly reached the conclusion that, armed with their "superior knowledge," they should run the world. They envisioned a society in which government and psychiatry would mutually serve one another. They concluded that psychiatry must become an indispensable part of the everyday functioning of government—Communist, fascist, democratic, it didn't particularly matter what kind of government, they could all benefit from and serve the ends of psychiatry—and to a very large extent over the next forty years, they accomplished that goal.

To learn about this strange conference, I spent a good deal of time talking to various civil rights groups and reading up on the growing volume of literature on psychiatric abuse. It seems that, beginning sometime in the early '70s, a very real backlash against the power of organized psychiatry had risen in the United States. Psychiatrists like Thomas Szasz and Peter Breggin were vocally challenging the basic assumptions of psychiatry (Szasz had gone so far as to question the very existence of mental illness). Civil liberties lawyers like San Francisco's Bruce Ennis were specializing in the defense of civil commitment cases and publishing studies of the subject (*The Prisoners of Psychiatry*). Citizen groups like the Network Against Psychiatric Assault and the Citizens Commission on Human Rights in Los Angeles were busy interviewing patients, looking over the shoulders of individual psychiatrists, and studying the political and social influence of the country's mental health organizations.

To all of these groups, the International Congress on Mental Hygiene was considered something of a grand conspiracy that set the guidelines for decades of arrogant abuse. They contend that, over the following years, laws were drafted that gave psychiatry a barrage of unlimited and unconstitutional powers—not only in the United States, Nazi Germany, and Soviet Russia, but in every

179

"civilized" country in the world (in South Africa, for instance, a bill was introduced that would make even the criticism of psychiatry an illegal offense). Although the phenomenon of mental illness was a complete mystery and the psychiatrists themselves could not even agree on its classifications (since the term *schizophrenia* was coined in 1911 it has had a thousand different meanings to a thousand different psychiatrists), they seemed to convince everyone that their right to classification should be unchallenged. Psychiatry gained the extraordinary power to arrest, detain, and sentence any citizen to an indefinite confinement without due process. The mere accusation of insanity was all it took for the suspension of every single human right guaranteed under the Constitution.

Whether or not there was actually an overt conspiracy between Seattle politicians and specific psychiatrists to incarcerate Frances Farmer in 1944, I do not know. Given the political climate and the people involved, it seems very possible. But the commitment laws were written so that they didn't really need to conspire to put her away. Mental illness is statutorily defined as "want of mental health" or "social deviance." In terms of the city of Seattle, Frances Farmer—like Marion Zioncheck and thousands of others—had been socially deviant all her life and, mad or not, that "difference" was all it took to bring her under the immensely powerful and very legal thumb of organized psychiatry.

36

While searching through Dr. Nicholson's yellowing and dusty papers, something I had been actively pursuing for over a year and a half finally turned up—a detailed record of the commitment proceeding against Frances Farmer.

It was incomplete and told entirely from Nicholson's point of view, but it is the only firsthand account that exists today. It states that on the morning of March 23, 1944, Frances was taken from the Harborview psychiatric ward, led to a small room in an adjacent ward, and seated before Dr. Nicholson and another psychiatrist, Dr. George Price.

There is no evidence that her guardian *ad litem*, Charles Stone, ever even spoke to her. This young attorney, who was an alcoholic and in no condition to defend anyone, merely signed a form waiving Frances' right to a jury trial—an incredible action in a case involving the involuntary commitment of a public figure. Exactly what Stone's motives were and why he refused to offer a defense are not known—when I spoke to his friends and relatives, I learned only that in later guilt-ridden years he refused to discuss the case, right up to the day in

181

1958 that he committed suicide in the garage of his family home.

I drove up to Harborview Hospital to get some idea of how the proceeding must have looked to Frances. That morning, thirty years later, they were having another commitment hearing for another Seattle woman. The sterile little room (and the fast and businesslike procedure) was virtually unchanged. As I sat in the back and watched, I got a sense of the terror and extraordinary indignity Frances must have felt in this situation. She had no idea of who these people were or what was going to happen next. She had not spoken to a lawyer, been informed of her rights, or given the slightest indication of *why* she was there in the first place.

Nicholson asked her a series of unrelated questions, which she answered with a good deal of resistance. On the commitment form where the examiner must indicate the evidence of mental unsoundness, he noted that:

—When asked how she slept in the hospital she said she tussled all night and heard voices that kept her awake.

—When asked if she lost weight, she slapped one of the examiners in the abdomen and said it looked as if he could lose some weight.

—In conversation, she referred to one of the examiners as "Polkadot" (presumably because of his necktie).

—She quoted poetry.

—She was vulgar and profane.

182

—She said she thought the examiners should be examined, not her.

On the form, under "Abnormal behavior noted," Nicholson wrote that she was "excited, arrogant, and inclined to be resistive." He wrote that she became "exceedingly vulgar and profane" in the examination and had been "vulgar to a high degree" since she had been at Harborview, using "vulgar" words that shocked and embarrassed the staff. She was, in short, suffering from schizophrenia. He signed a paper which said he had "heard the testimony of the witnesses, and personally examined Mrs. F. E. Anderson in reference to the charge of insanity and finds that said person is insane."

With that pen stroke, Frances lost every right she had ever known under the law. Since she had no money, Judge Frater ordered her to the Western Washington State Hospital for the Insane at Steilacoom. Two attendents grabbed her, put her in a straitjacket, and walked her down the stairs. One of the nurses on duty that day remembers that a large crowd had gathered in the halls of Harborview to watch the show. With a look of terror and disbelief on her face, Frances screamed out to the crowd to help her. Not one person budged as she was thrown into an ambulance and carried away.

37

The Western Washington State Hospital at Steilacoom is located on the site of the oldest settlement in the State of Washington, just south of Tacoma at the southern end of Puget Sound. In Indian fighting days it had been an army post (a young Ulysses S. Grant was among those garrisoned there at one time), and the ancient wooden buildings of the old fort remained, comprising the back wards of the insane asylum. Fort Steilacoom was not then (and is not now) a private sanitarium like La Cresenta. It was not tree-lined and grassy and peaceful. In the best of times it was overcrowded, understaffed, and inadequately financed. With the war on, Steilacoom's normally shocking conditions had gotten worse than even its worse critics could have imagined possible.

When I first drove up to this institution in mid-1975, the very sight of it was forbidding. The wards were situated in huge, dark, prisonlike buildings perpetually suspended in the rain and mist that rolls in off Puget Sound. I walked up to the main administration building and spoke to the head of the hospital. He seemed irritated and uninterested. He said the Farmer case was a "long time ago" and

184

there were no doctors remaining from those old days. He said no one in the present administration knew anything about it. But I was free to look at whatever records there were, and I was able to find several old-timers on the staff who remembered Frances and her first commitment there fairly well.

She arrived at Steilacoom late in the afternoon of March 24, 1944. She was taken from the padded van and led to the main receiving area. The straitjacket was removed and she was stripped. Standing nude before a large crowd of patients and orderlies that had assembled to see her, she was then numbered and fingerprinted. It was logged that the total amount of her personal property at the time of her commitment consisted of various articles of wearing apparel, one radio, and fifty books on different subjects. After this brief and humiliating reception ceremony, she was tied to a toilet for several minutes, and then—still nude—taken to a large bare auditorium-like room where about twenty-five sobbing and screaming patients paced about aimlessly or crouched on bare wooden benches that lined the four walls. She spent the night in this room, huddled in a corner for protection.

Early the next morning, she was taken to another, smaller room, where she was to begin immediately an extensive program of ETC (electroconvulsive shock) treatments. This new procedure, which at the time was standard for treating schizophrenia, depression, and even simple neurosis, had been devised just five years before by two Italians who got the idea from watching a pig go into convulsion after being accidentally electrocuted.

The technique consists of passing 70 to 130 volts of electricity through a patient's temples for 1/10 to 5/10 second, just long enough to induce convulsions and coma, on the theory that the patient's disordered brain will somehow rally in the face of such a massive trauma. (The unfortunate side effect of electroshock is that it destroys brain cells and can cause years of headache, disorientation, exhaustion, and permanent memory loss, and a considerable movement has risen in recent years to totally outlaw it.) Two attendants grabbed Frances and stretched her out in a prone position on a table in the center of the room. They attached electrodes to each of her temples and shoved a gag in her mouth. Then they stood back, turned on the electricity, and watched her body jump and twitch violently and uncontrollably until she passed out.

There is no way of knowing exactly what else happened during this initial confinement in 1944. The records are scanty and, as always, eyewitness versions are contradictory. But Frances had a reputation for being the most angry, rebellious inmate in the asylum. She refused to cooperate with the psychiatrists. She refused to admit she had a mental problem. She screamed that she was being unjustly incarcerated and demanded to be released. The stubborn independence and integrity that had made her a successful artist were here deemed "antisocial" behavior and she was treated for it with massive weekly doses of electroshock. When even this failed to get a response, she was given hydrotherapy, a primitive form of shock treatment (now outlawed) in which she was stripped naked and thrown into a tub of icy water for six to eight hours and during which she very nearly chewed off her lower lip.

Months of such treatment went by and Frances' resistance gradually melted. She became, she would write some time later, "like a bowl of jelly, agreeable and pliable." She seemed to become almost another person. ("I'm sorry," she supposedly told the doctors. "I was rude and disrespectful. I was very, very sick.") She flattered the nurses and orderlies. She admitted the error in her thinking. She became a model patient. The doctors immediately announced that she was completely cured. "Frances has responded to treatment and made a remarkable recovery," they told the press. Edwin J. Alexander, Supervisor of Deportations [i.e., extradition], announced: "Dr. W. N. Keller, superintendent of Western State Hospital, advises me that Frances Farmer has made a complete recovery, and that in his opinion she will not have a relapse. We are therefore discontinuing the deportation proceedings initiated by the La Crescenta institution against her." And in Seattle, Dr. Donald Nicholson told an audience: "I think this case demonstrates just how successfully antisocial behavior can be modified. Three months ago this woman was totally unresponsive and today she is being returned to her family completely cured. This marks a significant victory for the mental hygiene movement in Washington State."

38

Frances was officially paroled from Steilacoom on the morning of July 2, 1944. Before
her release, however, a court order had been
prepared naming her mother as her legal guardian.
This order was more far-reaching and restrictive
than has ever been placed on even the most incorri-
gible of criminal parolees. She would not be able to
see friends or seek employment or even leave the
house without her mother's permission. The order
quite literally gave Lillian Farmer complete control
over every aspect of her life.

The very day she got home, her mother called
a press conference to announce publicly "the return
of Frances Farmer." Reporters from the Seattle
papers were welcomed to the house to inspect her
sanity. Frances smiled through it. Would she return
to Hollywood to resume her career, they asked?
Indeed she would. What exactly had been her
problem? Overwork. How had she found her experience at the Steilacoom institution? Mrs. Farmer
interrupted to say that the doctor's work there was
"almost miraculous."

A large stack of fan mail was presented and
Frances was photographed reading through it. ("It's

188

a little sad," she said, "to think that people are so lonely that they'll sit down and write to people they've never met. But, of course, fan mail is the lifeblood of an actress—if you stop getting it, you know you're through.") She was so gracious and cooperative that the press went away satisfied that Frances was indeed a new person and perhaps could make a comeback in the movies after all. With several glowing pictures to prove it, the *Post-Intelligencer* reported that Frances was finally "normal":

> Completely cured from the breakdown which interrupted her screen career last summer, Frances Farmer was back home in Seattle yesterday preparing to essay a comeback at the earliest possible moment.
>
> And she's confident that she has a good chance—because, despite the fact she's been under treatment in the Western State Hospital at Steilacoom for the last three months, she knows she still has a public. That was made clear by the stack of fan mail she found awaiting her when she arrived at her parents' home at 2636 47th SW.
>
> Miss Farmer appeared to be in glowing health and said she had never felt better in her life. She had put on fifteen pounds at the hospital—but the added weight didn't make her any less photogenic.
>
> "I'm anxious to get back to work just as soon as I can," she said. "Of course my future is

very vague, as yet—I haven't anything defi-
nite in mind. It all depends on what opportu-
nities I get."

She had a new "upswept" hairdo, which
made her look for all the world like a Gibson
girl of a half century ago.

"It just happened to fall that way," she said.
"I like to try different ways of doing my hair.
Sometimes, if you get old-fashioned enough,
you find you're modern."

Miss Farmer, who is thirty, is a University of
Washington graduate. She was at the height
of her stardom when she collapsed under the
strain of overwork last year. . . . Her mother
was compelled to have her committed to
Steilacoom when she failed to respond to
home treatment for what was diagnosed as a
"split personality."

The next day Frances ran away. Her mother
called the police and had her returned before she got
past the city limits. Her father then took her to
Nevada to stay at the Smith Valley ranch home of
her aunt (Lillian's sister) Mrs. Edith Castaing. When
they got to Reno, Frances ran off again and was returned by the police again. It seemed she was in a
double bind, a dilemma without solution. She had
received enough electroshock treatment to make a
vegetable out of a lesser person, and she was obviously frightened and terribly disoriented. But she
knew she didn't want to go back to Hollywood and
resume a broken career, and she knew she didn't

want to go back to Steilacoom. She also knew that with her mother as legal guardian she was going to end up doing one of the two. She was a prisoner and, like all prisoners, the only thing she could think of was escape.

On July 15, 1944, she ran away from her aunt's house and got as far as Antioch, California, where she was promptly arrested as a vagrant. This time the press got wind of the story and the arrest made national headlines. Reporters from all over the country descended upon the Antioch police station to witness the final degradation of a great Hollywood star. Chief of police Al Leroy held a news conference to tell of how he recognized and single-handedly captured her. She was led before the reporters and photographers wearing ragged dungarees held up by a rope belt. The Associated Press reported:

> Disclosure that blond Frances Farmer, former motion-picture star, has been the object of a secret search since her disappearance from a Reno, Nev., hotel July 15, was made yesterday by her mother, Mrs. Lillian V. Farmer.
>
> Meanwhile, the blond, blue-eyed actress was held in "protective custody" by Antioch, Calif., police.
>
> Shabbily garbed as a fruit picker, she later appeared before Justice of the Peace Tom Milan, where she identified herself as the former film star. Judge Milan reportedly fined her $10 on a vagrancy count....

191

Chief of police Al Leroy of Antioch reported the girl could give no address when she was taken into custody here. It was said she had been seeking work in the fruit orchards near Antioch.

At the same time, the former actress' agent in Hollywood yesterday reported that she had been offered a starring role in a film production of *The Enchanted Forest* but had made no response.

What was not reported—and would not come out until I sent someone to talk to the people of that dusty little town all those years later—was that Frances had desperately and angrily tried to explain herself. She told them that she did not want to be a Hollywood star. She said the plight of migrant workers had always been one of her major concerns and she wanted to work the fruit orchards just for the experience ("I *need* to work," she had insisted). She tried to tell them that she was not crazy, that her family and the city of Seattle were persecuting her and she was just trying to get away and live her own life—which, of course, only convinced them she was about as crazy as it was humanly possible to be.

192

39

I tried to find someone Frances might have communicated with after the Antioch fiasco—some friend or relative to whom she might have confided the extraordinary circumstances of her plight—but there was apparently no one. After Antioch, Frances seems to have given up any hope of getting away for at least a while. Her father came over from Reno and drove her back to her aunt's house in Nevada Hot Springs and she withdrew deep into herself. She stayed around the house a virtual prisoner, saying almost nothing, refusing to read her mail, but generally accepting her fate. She spent her days reading, sunning, and teaching children's swimming classes in her aunt's pool, and her nights staring intently at the wall in her room trying to patch the large gaps in her memory from the intensive electroshock treatments.

Lillian Farmer seems to have been very optimistic about Frances' condition at this point. Within days of Antioch she had called the press and told them Frances was "just fine—physically and mentally. She is in excellent spirits and in good hands, staying with my sister, Mrs. Edith Castaing. My sister is a former nurse, you know. They are at

193

Nevada Hot Springs, about seven miles from Yer-rington. My daughter is teaching children to swim—getting plenty of health-giving outdoor exer-cise. . . . Frances has picture offers, but I don't want her to plunge into that work too soon. She's been away from it a long time and it's so strenuous. I want her to stay here until she is thoroughly rested—and strong."

As for Frances' father's attitude, he said lit-tle. He obviously loved his daughter very much and had always been enormously proud of her ac-complishments. He was concerned enough to reenter her life periodically during this time. But he was an almost pathologically ineffectual man where his family was concerned. He was thoroughly intimi-dated by his wife and it was very easy for him to believe that Frances was sick. After all, he had read the newspaper accounts and he could *see* that she was not herself. He actually appears to have been rather frightened of her, and after he brought her back from Antioch—a trip in which father and daughter barely spoke to one another—he hurried back to Seattle with a sigh of relief.

Frances remained in Nevada for the next six months, under what must have been for her ex-tremely difficult conditions. She was not allowed to see anyone or read anything that might "upset" her. Every movement, every nuance in her voice was watched carefully for an indication of a "relapse." Most difficult of all was the fact that she was never allowed to be alone. Finally, on January 13, 1945, she could stand this kind of preventive detention no longer. While she and her aunt were in Reno on a shopping trip, she ran off again. She was the object of a major police search before she was captured, hiding out in a Reno movie theater a few hours later watching a movie (Headline: 'FRANCES FARMER DISAPPEARS AGAIN, IS FOUND'). The next day the police escorted her back to Nevada Hot Springs.

Back in Seattle, the doctors of Steilacoom had been watching all this activity very closely. Frances had been pronounced "completely cured" with a great deal of fanfare, and professional reputations were on the line. Once again, this woman was being an embarrassment to the city of Seattle—making a national spectacle of herself by running away and getting herself arrested for vagrancy. Representatives of both the Steilacoom institution and the county psychopathic division began contacting Mrs. Farmer and telling her that Frances had, in effect, tricked them. She had merely been "acting" normal and her rebellious spirit had not been broken. She had obviously needed "more treatment" all along.

What happened next defies any kind of rational explanation. During the first few months of 1945, Frances began to recover from her shock treatments and was even beginning to get over her rather understandable paranoia. She was feeling so much better by mid-April that her mother brought her back to Seattle. On April 27, Mrs. Farmer told the press that Frances' health was "much improved" and implied she would soon go to Hollywood. One week later, on May 5, 1945 at exactly 6:30 P.M., Frances left the house with a friend and drove down to Tacoma to visit some other old friends. She did not bother to ask her mother for permission. When Mrs. Farmer noticed that her daughter was gone, she called the police to search for her. She also called the *Post-Intelligencer* and made the following announcement:

> I asked for police assistance because I was terribly worried about Frances. She has never made a full recovery from her illness and will have to be hospitalized again soon.

When Frances got back a few hours later, her mother took one look at her, called the police, had her taken back to Steilacoom, and saw to it that she stayed there for the next five years.

40

Many years later, after her death in 1970, the autobiography of Frances Farmer would strongly maintain that during this period she had been subjected to inhuman treatment at this Washington State institution—giving a detailed account of sadistic guards and unsanitary conditions and patients who ate their own excrement. During the second half of 1975, when I finally began searching out the veterans of Steilacoom one by one, it became clear that these shocking descriptions hardly scratched the surface of what Frances actually experienced during this second commitment at the Western Washington State Hospital at Steilacoom.

Events occurred rapidly. She was powerless and had neither the time nor the knowledge to assess what was happening to her. As a recidivist, she was not granted a reevaluation of her sanity. Patients with a history of readmission were simply considered incurable. A quick hearing (at which she was not present) was held by King County Hospital Superintendent A. J. Hockett, ordering her recommitment. She was then immediately driven to Steilacoom, taken directly to the back barracks where the violent and hopelessly insane were housed. There

197

she was stripped, her nails cut to the quick, her head shaven, and she was thrown into a shrieking mob of naked mental patients.

There was nothing in her experience with mental institutions that could have possibly prepared her for the condition of the Steilacoom violent ward. The rotten wooden building was nearly a hundred years old and had never been even partially restored. The floors in the entire lower section were bare dirt. In this single area a crowded conglomeration of psychopathic criminals, hopeless catatonics, senile old people, and mentally retarded children were herded together, living off cots spaced no more than a foot apart—some chained to the cots, others curled up on the ground. There was no attempt at discipline or order in the ward. Food was thrown to the floor and the patients fought each other and the rats to get at it. Patients urinated and defecated and took sexual liberties with one another like caged animals in a crowded zoo. The only concession to sanitation was that every month or so—even in the dead of winter—patients were lined up outside and washed down with a powerful fire hose.

Over and over again people would tell of seeing the patients sexually degraded. The orderlies at Steilacoom were mostly trustee inmates of McNeil Island Federal Penitentiary across the Sound and, like those of many state institutions, they had turned their position into a lucrative pimping service. On almost any night of the year, soldiers from nearby Fort Lewis were sneaked in for clandestine sexual relations with female patients. ("Steilacoom," five

198

separate individuals would say, "was the whorehouse of Fort Lewis.") Frances was suddenly subjected to obscene perversions, raped by orderlies, friends of orderlies, and other patients hundreds of times. One of the most vivid recollections of some veterans of the institution would be the sight of Frances Farmer being held down by orderlies and raped by drunken gangs of soldiers.

A nurse named Nancy Lilly, who had worked on the ward in late 1945 and early 1946, tried to give me some idea of what Frances' life must have been like in those years. Since she was physically able she was put on work detail and for the most part her daily life was taken up with work—backbreaking work like cleaning up the piles of human waste and vomit that covered the floor after every feeding. When Frances refused to work—which was often—her punishment was an extended series of shock treatments. Week after week she was wheeled into the treatment room and jolted into insensibility, and each time she regained consciousness, she remained what the staff termed "unresponsive."

This was the truly amazing part of the first years of her confinement, the nurse said. They could not break her. Whatever quality it was that had brought her into lifelong conflict with the outside society, it had stiffened and matured and manifested itself in an incredible resistance to the institution. The records show that Frances remained as stubborn and uncooperative and bitterly sarcastic as she had been the day she entered the institution. She was very likely the most rebellious patient in the history of Steilacoom—she was so resistive that she became a kind of Ken Kesey heroine to many of the patients. No matter what was done to her, she refused to cooperate in any way or admit anything was getting to her.

The only time this nurse saw Frances deeply affected was one particular Christmas Day. The orderlies had taken Frances out of her ward, handed her a hospital gown, and led her to the main dining hall, the first time she had ever been permitted there. When she stepped into the room, she noticed a large group of staff and patients seated waiting for her, many of them grinning and holding back giggles. As she took her seat, the lights went off and a movie started. It was *Son of Fury*, and when Frances saw the images of herself in a beautiful dress and diamond tiara, languishing in the arms of Tyrone Power, she started screaming and she continued screaming and crying as she was put under restraint and carried all the way back to the violent ward.

41

The process of searching out and interviewing the veterans of Steilacoom went on for several more months. Nurses, orderlies, janitors, all seemed to want to talk about the things they had witnessed—even the head of the state department of health services confessed that those were "terrible, terrible" times. The doctors involved were more reluctant—many, in fact, would turn to stone at the mention of Frances' name—but, when pressed, they would usually say it was an "intriguing" or "particularly stubborn" case and then proceed to outline the fascinating little details of the treatments and procedures used on her. Everyone who had served at Steilacoom seemed to have a different Frances Farmer story, and put together, these stories formed the eerie picture of what appeared to be a concentrated psychiatric assault aimed at breaking down the resistance of one woman.

In the days right after World War II, the field of psychiatry was in the midst of the greatest boom in its history. An enormous mental health "consciousness" had arisen during the war—primarily due to publicity dealing with the half-million reported cases of battle fatigue—which carried over

201

into peacetime and added immeasurably to the mystique and prestige of the profession. In 1946, President Harry Truman signed the National Mental Health Act, expanding the functions of the Mental Hygiene Division of the Public Health Service and further linking psychiatry with the everyday functionings of government. Organizations like the American Psychiatric Association, the Psychiatric Foundation, the National Mental Health Foundation, and the National Committee for Mental Hygiene grew and expanded their activities and developed enormous power and influence over every aspect of American life.

It was an extraordinary situation. The best that could be said about the practice of psychiatry up to that time was that it didn't work. Virtually every treatment, every theory, every term, would later be discredited and discarded as a total failure—the profession still could not even define mental illness except as "want of mental health." (Psychiatrists of the time were still writing scholarly treatises to the effect that masturbation causes schizophrenia.) And yet, psychiatry was being handed not only credibility but unquestioned power to suspend civil rights and classify and mold human behavior (just as had been outlined in the Washington Conference of 1930.) More important, the world at large was coming to accept its thesis that mental illness was the epidemic of modern times, that there would be an ever-increasing army of patients on the horizon, and that the discipline of psychiatry deserved to be able to use whatever means was necessary to combat it.

202

Within this ever-expanding world of psychiatry, the name of Frances Farmer had become notorious. Word of the stubborn case of the former movie queen had reached to psychiatric circles all over the country and had aroused enormous interest. She was the most famous personality ever to be committed to a public mental institution and her failure to respond had become both an embarrassment and an intriguing challenge to the entire profession. By early 1947, some of the most illustrious psychiatrists in the world were stopping by to inspect her, review her case, and offer help. She was variously (and meaninglessly) diagnosed as "paranoid," "schizophrenic," "manic-depressive," "catatonic," and as having a "split personality," depending on the doctor, and more series of radical treatments were advised.

The treatments that were recommended tended increasingly to make use of experimental drugs. Western State Hospital had begun a pioneering program aimed at developing a chemical means of controlling mental patients some months before, and Frances was eyed right from the start. Under the direction of Dr. William Keller and Dr. J. R. Shanklin, the head psychiatrists of Steilacoom, Frances was integrated into the program sometime in 1947. Practically every experimental drug that came along in that period was tested on her—most likely even LSD—and she had the distinction of being one of the first mental patients in the country to be treated with the immobilizing, antidepressant, behavior-modification, and mind-controlling drugs which within five years would become standard in the nation's mental hospitals—drugs the pharmaceutical companies would later give names like Thorazine, Stelazine, Mellaril, and Prolixin.

There is no existing record of how this drug program was administered. But it lasted for at least a year—one year of an unprecedented chemical assault on her mind and body. And yet, amazingly, the results were negative. The drugs were very effective in temporarily altering her behavior but they seemed to have no lasting effect on what was considered the basic manifestation of her mental illness—her rebellion against the authority of the institution. They simply could not seem to break her spirit of resistance. For that they would have to take even more drastic measures.

42

The year 1947 was the very beginning of what would later be known as the McCarthy Era. The House un-American Activities Committee had just been reactivated in Washington, D.C., and was starting to look into Communist activities in Hollywood. The Northwest was already engulfed in a hysteria of anti-Communism unequaled since the mid-'30s. There was a genuine fear in the air and any people with the slightest hint of radical leanings in their background, or the faintest association with such famous Northwest radical figures as Frances Farmer, Anna Louise Strong, or Marion Zioncheck, were suddenly trying to hide it. (Frances' old high school teacher and chief supporter Belle McKenzie was among the first to be hounded into seclusion.)

In the midst of all this, on the morning of October 20, 1947, a reporter for the *Seattle Times* named Ed Guthman drove out to West Seattle to do a special interview with Mrs. Lillian V. Farmer. Mrs. Farmer had called the *Times* city editor and told him that there was a great hidden political angle behind the Frances Farmer tragedy that had never been even hinted at in the press. She said that the political climate had finally changed to the point that she could tell the story without fear for her life. She said that if they would send a reporter she would finally divulge that incredible true story to the people of Seattle and close the book on Frances Farmer once and for all.

Guthman found the old Farmer house in a badly run-down condition, the paint peeling and the yard desperately in need of attention. Mrs. Farmer, now a wrinkled cronelike figure in her mid-seventies, greeted him at the door and sat him down in front of the big stone living room fireplace where Frances had once posed for publicity photographs. She told him that the untold truth behind Frances' tragedy was that she had been an agent of world Communism all her life. She told him that Frances had been indoctrinated into Communist circles as a student and had been used, tricked, and coerced by them until they broke her down all the way. "Men who were admitted Communists and who had influence in New York and Hollywood held some terrible threat over her," she said. "Frances would never say what it was, but the Communists were able to make her do things she didn't want to do. They were continually after her for money and when she tried to break away, they frightened her into her present mental state."

She related how Frances had been influenced by radical teaching while a student at West Seattle High. "It was all done so subtly" she said. "Somehow Frances was taught to sneer at American traditions and to admire Russia's five-year plan which was then in operation. She came home from school with beliefs that the Constitution was outmoded

206

and our government a farce. At the university, Frances was even encouraged to attend Communist meetings. . . . It is not a pretty story and I've hesitated a long time to tell it, but what happened to Frances has happened and is happening to other talented, sensitive young people. Perhaps the telling of her experiences will save others from being drawn by the Communists' false promises."

She told how Frances trusted the Communists and how they used her as an attraction at meetings and on moneymaking tours. She said that Frances was an entertainer for such organizations as the American Youth Congress and the American League for Peace and Democracy, and that she was connected to many other Communist-front organizations. "They interfered in her public and private life. I attended some of the meetings with her and it was always some moneymaking scheme. I don't know how much Frances gave them, but it would run well into the thousands of dollars. When she finally realized that Communism in truth was a plot against our country, she tried to break away. When I asked her why she couldn't, she replied, 'Mom, I've had access to their meetings and I guess I've seen too much . . .' When she tried to escape, they kept her from getting parts in movies, were instrumental in breaking up her marriage to Leif Erickson, and blackmailed and threatened her at every opportunity."

Here, in a neat, concise statement, was Lillian Farmer's analysis of the conspiracy against her daughter (an analysis which, incidently her other daughter Edith vehemently shares right up to the

207

present time). It seemed unlikely, but it had to be checked out. I called the reporter Guthman, who had gone on to become a Pulitzer Prize-winner and National Editor of the *Los Angeles Times*. He said he didn't remember much about her charges except that they seemed a rather typical paranoid outburst of the McCarthy era. I went back and rechecked all my sources on Frances' connection with radical politics. There was no evidence that I could turn up to even hint at any kind of Communist campaign against her.

But for Lillian Farmer, this theory was perfect justification for everything she had done and believed regarding Frances. All their lives, these two strong-willed women had been locked in an obsessive struggle, while at the same time strangely seeking each other's support and approval. In the course of this struggle, Frances had rebelled against her mother's most cherished values. She had embraced the very things her mother most feared and hated. She had been warned, and time and again she had laughed at that warning and—just look!—the absolute worst had happened. Now, in the seventy-fifth year of her life, with her daughter's subjugation nearly complete and her paranoia suddenly being reinforced all around her, Lillian Farmer could feel that she had been totally vindicated. She had won the struggle with her daughter. And as I read through her statement over and over again I could detect between those lines an unmistakable sense of—and there is no other word for it—satisfaction.

43

I was not able to learn much about Frances'
day-to-day life during the year 1948. There
are strong and persistent rumors that she was
packed off to various mental institutions around the
country and poked and prodded like some exotic
laboratory specimen—but I could find no real evidence of it. There are almost no surviving medical
records and only a handful of people who even saw
her in that year. The only thing that these people
agree on is that she somehow managed to remain the
most rebellious and unmanageable inmate in the
asylum. Every psychological injustice made her
more angry, every treatment made her more stubborn, and, in the end, every experimental drug
failed to break her.

But even though there is no way of knowing
exactly what transpired at Steilacoom during that
year, we do know the quality of life at that institution: There are detailed records showing that the
overall physical situation there had deteriorated to
the point of utter chaos. The postwar psychiatric
boom had resulted in a near doubling of civil commitments (by 1948, some 250,000 commitments a
year were taking place, which meant that one out of

209

every two patients in a hospital bed was there because he or she had been classified a mental patient), and public mental institutions simply couldn't handle the load. In Steilacoom, the wards had become so drastically overcrowded and understaffed—2,736 patients crammed into fourteen wards, supervised by a mere handful of attendants—that it was scarcely able to function at all. The ancient wooden buildings were crumbling with dry rot and old age. The previous year, a massive fire had destroyed one of the buildings, killing a number of patients and making the wards even more crowded. A researcher who was making the rounds of state mental hospitals at the time noted: "In some of the wards there were scenes that rivaled the horrors of the Nazi concentration camps—hundreds of naked mental patients herded into huge, barnlike, filth-infested wards, in all degrees of deterioration, untended and untreated, stripped of every vestige of human decency, many in stages of semistarvation."

It would be comforting to believe that no one knew about these conditions—certainly no intimate of Frances—but it is simply not true. Stories about Steilacoom were running rampant at that time. In late 1948, a social affairs reporter for the *Seattle Post-Intelligencer* named Lucille Cohen began hearing so many reports that Steilacoom was being run like some kind of concentration camp that she began a personal investigation. Though she was never allowed to see the violent ward—where the conditions were so much worse—and never got close to Frances Farmer, her investigation confirmed even the wildest of these reports. On February 18, 1949, she even wrote a long muckraking article that appeared under a page-one banner headline:

> Drastic overcrowding and understaffing at the big state mental hospital at Steilacoom was laid bare today.
>
> Dr. W. N. Keller, hospital superintendent, confirmed the serious situation uncovered by the *Post-Intelligencer*. . . .
>
> Patients are sleeping in unheated courts, a canvas covering over apertures their only protection from the weather. . . . Some of the beds in the courts have to be protected by rubber covers from soaking on rainy days.
>
> In inside wards, beds are jammed one next to the other.
>
> The hospital has fifteen graduate nurses for its 2,736 patients [augmented by] twenty-three student nurses from the University of Washington.
>
> Bad living quarters for staff complicate the problem of getting efficient help. Six night ward attendents are housed in a basement with sagging floors, crumbling cement walls, and ceilings honeycombed with uncovered pipes. . . .

This page-one story laid those conditions out for the people of Washington to see, and for a while, at least, it looked as if it would cause a serious reexamination of the entire state mental health system.

211

But in the end it turned out to be just so much talk. Cohen got a journalism award. Politicians came out and stated that they deplored such conditions. The state supervisor of institutions defended Steilacoom by declaring that Washington's institutions were no worse than those of other states. Dr. Keller cried out that there was a serious national shortage of psychiatrists and an international epidemic of mental illness and the simple solution to Steilacoom's problem was more money and more and better psychiatrists. And before long everyone tired of talking about it, the problems of the Cold War moved the story off page one, and within a few months it was completely forgotten.

While I was going through Lucille Cohen's papers (she died in a house fire in 1960), one of the former University of Washington student nurses she had mentioned in her article sought me out and told me a curious story. It was forbidden, she said, for student nurses to go to the back wards. But she was only nineteen years old and very determined to see the movie star she had idolized as a child. One day she wandered off to the forbidden wards to try and catch a glimpse of Frances Farmer. She saw the dirt floors, the patients chained to beds, the vomit and unspeakable sanitary conditions, and finally, was able to find Frances. She said she actually spoke to her and even held an intelligible conversation. She eventually came back several times and each time spoke with her. The nurse said she became convinced that Frances was neither paranoid schizophrenic nor catatonic (as she was then diagnosed),

212

and wrote out a full report for the superintendent to tell him so:

> The patient is highly intelligent and aware of what is going on around her. Patient's rebelliousness seems to be due to her present circumstances. Patient lives in substandard sanitary environment and lacks proper diet. Staff is unnecessarily brutal to patient. . . .

The nurse was immediately censured for insubordination and transferred to another hospital. She wrote the newspapers and even her Congressman and told them her story and never received so much as a written reply. All those years later, she would remember Frances as a "saint," a woman with a "rugged determination to maintain her dignity." Even there, in those conditions, she was beautiful, she said, so unbelievably beautiful. "Pictures just don't do justice to her. You don't know how beautiful she was unless you saw her in person."

213

44

One morning in early June, 1975, while I was still knee-deep in Steilacoom records, Frances' sister Edith came to Seattle to see me. She had called earlier from Portland and said she had something important she wanted to show me. I met her in the newspaper lobby at about 10:30. We exchanged greetings, rather awkwardly I recall, and went to the cafeteria to have coffee.

She was a short, attractive, seemingly intelligent woman who looked nothing at all like her famous sister. I had been prepared not to like her (how could she have let this happen to her own sister?) but I ended up being very taken with her. For nearly three hours we sat there and talked about the mysteries of Frances Farmer. She told me family anecdotes and showed me pictures of Frances as a child and in the years just before her death. She also showed me the manuscript of a book she was writing about Frances ("in the context of a family history") called *My Sister Frances: A Look Back with Love.*

There was not much she could tell me about Frances that I didn't already know. Edith had been out of the country during most of these events and seemed to know nothing about the specifics of the commitment. Her main purpose in seeing me, it turned out, was to gain evidence to prove the autobiography of her sister was a fraud. ("That book was a libel against my whole family," she said, "and I know for a fact that Frances didn't write a word of it.") As she spoke, it began to dawn on me how helpless and perplexed—not to mention guilty—she must have felt in the face of this enormous family tragedy; like her mother she was utterly convinced "the Communists" were behind the entire thing. She could look me right in the eye and say: "The life of Frances Farmer is an inspiring story of how a talented and beautiful Hollywood star, bogged down in personal problems, nonetheless fought off the attempts of Communists who wanted to make her one of their own."

But Edith was able to give me some interesting secondhand information about the various treatments given Frances at Steilacoom and some of the "strange things" that had happened to her there. She said that her mother had not wanted the doctors to use those drastic treatments on Frances and they had been administered without her knowledge or permission. She said she knew Frances had been given many "experimental drugs" and had been the subject of several medical experiments. And then, just as she was getting up to leave, she told me a very interesting story.

She said that one day toward the end of Frances' confinement in Steilacoom, her father had gone to visit her. While he was waiting in the reception area to see Dr. Keller, the head of the hospital,

215

he got into conversation with one of the doctors. The doctor calmly mentioned to him that Frances was a hopeless case and let it slip that they were "going to be giving her a lobotomy soon." On hearing this, Mr. Farmer went to Dr. Keller and objected strenuously. He called his brother (Dr. Frank Farmer, a physician in California) and asked him to write Dr. Keller a letter threatening a lawsuit if they went ahead with the operation ("stopping them," Edith said, "cold in their tracks").

There were several things about the story that bothered me. According to her records, Frances began "responding" to treatment sometime in the first part of 1949 and was released as cured in early 1950. Yet, as of late 1948, she was being considered absolutely incurable. She was so "hopeless" that they wanted to perform a lobotomy. Something had obviously happened in the space of a few short months in late 1948 or early 1949 to change their diagnosis. Either the doctors had had a miraculous change of attitude or they had done something drastic to Frances (that no one knew about) to warrant her release. But what? Several people had mentioned "lobotomy" in the past, but it seemed impossible. She had no visible scars on her head. She had not been left a complete vegetable, the most frequent result of such an operation. Then what could have happened to make the doctors change their minds so suddenly?

The answer to that question seemed to be the key to the remaining mystery of Frances Farmer. Was it possible that someone at Steilacoom had performed the operation without permission? It was a provocative thought and not inconceivable—especially considering the fact they didn't seem to feel they needed permission for any of the other radical treatments. But what would account for the lack of a scar or of vegetablelike behavior? I didn't have the slightest idea of what it all meant until one day several weeks later when my phone rang. Suddenly there on the line was a man who claimed to know everything there was to know about the Frances Farmer insanity case.

Over the past few years I had spoken to hundreds of cranks and obvious psychotics and I was never sure of how much to believe when I got these calls. This man seemed to know a lot of intimate details of the case, so for about a half an hour or so I listened to his version of the psychiatric confinement of his favorite movie star. He said his name was Alan Dobson and he had been a journalist who covered the story for the AP in the late '40s and early '50s. He said he had actually interviewed Frater and Nicholson and even followed Frances into Steilacoom at one point. His contention—which everyone ridiculed at the time—was that the U.S. Government and the entire psychiatric establishment of the country had cooperated to "remake" Frances Farmer. He said they had wanted to demonstrate how effective psychiatry could modify the behavior of even the most notorious troublemaker—essentially as part of the now famous CIA psychiatric experimental program of the same period. He sounded, frankly, rather paranoid on the subject and I didn't take what he said too seriously. But before he hung up, he said

something rather intriguing. He said he was sure
the final step for Frances at Steilacoom had to do
with something or somebody named "Freeman."

45

It was some time before I could make any sense out of what this man was trying to tell me. Someone suggested that perhaps he meant the name of a clinic or a particular doctor who had treated her. The first was unlikely—there was no Freeman Hospital—but to check out the latter I went to see a friend who was doing research for various human rights organizations. When I threw out the name "Freeman," he recognized it immediately. Walter Freeman had been simply America's foremost (and most infamous) psychosurgeon.

The very recognition of his name seemed to turn loose a torrent of information about those last months Frances spent at Steilacoom. Newspaper accounts showed that Dr. Freeman had indeed visited the Western State Hospital late in the year 1948—in order to conduct a series of experimental neurological operations. When I requestioned veterans of the institution, they knew all about the famous doctor and admitted that, yes, he had been very interested in Frances Farmer. Eventually, I found detailed accounts and even a series of photographs documenting his experiments at Steilacoom and, when put together, they told an almost

219

unbelievable story, hidden for over twenty-five years.

It began in 1935, some five years after the famous Washington Psychiatric Conference. One of the conference delegates, a Portuguese neurologist named Egar Moniz, in that year developed a method of surgically severing certain organically undamaged portions of the brain to effect startling modifications in behavior. In a series of experiments on social misfits provided by the Portuguese Government, he found he could enter the human brain and, by remarkably simple surgical means, duplicate the results of years of slower, less radical treatment. The procedure—which he called a prefrontal lobotomy—worked particularly well with people with "obsessive syndromes" and "anxiety-tension states," especially people of high intelligence, women, children, and rebellious adolescents. And its potential in the treatment of schizophrenics, alcoholics, homosexuals, and even political radicals was thought to be truly revolutionary. When the profession of psychiatry came into real power in the late '40s, it seized upon this method as the "ultimate" treatment. In 1949, Moniz was awarded the Nobel Prize for Medicine, and that same year tens of thousands of lobotomies were performed around the world.

In the United States, the most enthusiastic practitioner of this dramatic new method was Dr. Walter Freeman, head of the neurology department of Georgetown University in Washington, D.C. Freeman had studied with Moniz and had been, in fact, the first person to perform a lobotomy in the

United States. His texts (*Psychosurgery, Psychosurgery and the Self*) would become the standard works in the field, and his research had already earned him a reputation as "the father of American lobotomy." The same year that the procedure was first gaining wide acceptance—1947—Freeman had come forward with an entirely different "transorbital" approach to the operation, with which he felt he was getting miraculous results and which he felt had revolutionary possibilities not only for psychiatry but for the future of mankind.

The transorbital lobotomy was a simpler and much cleaner form of surgery than the older style of prefrontal lobotomy, and involved considerably less risk of leaving the patient in a vegetablelike state. In Freeman's version of the operation, the surgeon would enter the brain under the eyelid and work directly on the portion of the brain associated with violent and rebellious tendencies, without so much as leaving a scar. The operation was performed by inserting a thin calibrated instrument, resembling an icepick, between the patient's eye and eyelid, and driving it through the orbital plate and into the brain to a final depth of about $1\frac{1}{2}$ inches, where it was moved only slightly to sever the nerves connecting the cortex with the thalamus. The whole operation could be performed in less than a few minutes, with not a good deal more fuss than the administration of a penicillin shot. Freeman was absolutely convinced that when his technique was fully developed, he could surgically "control" schizophrenia, habitual criminality, homosexuality, habitual masturbation, and practically every other deviation that has ever

221

plagued society; and of all the state mental hospitals in the country in which to conduct the experiments that would insure its proper development, he choose the Western Washington State Hospital at Steilacoom.

Freeman made a number of sojourns to Western State altogether—first in late 1947, then again in 1948, and finally sometime in 1949. The famous doctor was an imposing figure—a large balding man with a Viennese goatee and steel-rimmed glasses— and each time he was treated like visiting royalty by the psychiatrists of Western State, who followed him around, hanging on his every word (and who, many years later when this operation became regarded as little more than a medical atrocity, would refuse to admit they had anything to do with him). Like many brilliant surgeons, Freeman had both colossal arrogance and a natural flair for showmanship. At Spencer State Hospital in Spencer, West Virginia, he had once lobotomized thirty-five women patients at one time in a test of what he called "mass surgery." He enjoyed having an audience while he worked, and he frequently boasted of the number of lobotomies he had performed (one thousand) on both the hopelessly insane and on sane people with "neurological illness." On his second trip to Steilacoom, in a room packed with visiting psychiatrists, he performed lobotomies on thirteen women in a row, explaining the philosophy behind his technique as he worked:

> The patients for whom this operation brings the best results are those who are tortured

222

with self-concern, who suffer from terribly painful disabling self-consciousness, whether it expresses itself in pains in the body organs or terrible distress from feelings of persecution. . . . In ordinary language, the technique severs the nerves that deliver emotional power to ideas. Along with a cure comes some loss in the patient's imaginative power. But that's what we want to do. They are sick in their imaginations. . . .

Like so many other psychiatrists, Freeman had long been fascinated by the case of Frances Farmer. She was the most celebrated person ever to be confined to a U.S. public mental institution and very likely the main reason he had come to Steilacoom in the first place. He had examined her at least three times over the months, found her defiant and uncooperative, and determined that, yes, she was hopelessly sick in her imagination.

Toward the end of this second visit—at the very end of 1948—Freeman had Frances brought before him in a remote treatment room. She was placed on a table and administered electric shock until she passed out. All the nurses and orderlies then filed out of the room. No one will ever know exactly what happened next, but the overwhelming conclusion drawn by the people of Steilacoom at the time was that the doctor lifted her right eyelid and stuck a needle into her brain. Because when she came to, Frances Farmer was not the same person she had been, and she would never be the same person again.

46

For the first time in nearly ten years, Frances seemed to respond to her psychiatric "treatment." As she recuperated over the following months, her attitude miraculously began to change. All the old rebellion drained out of her. Her resistance crumbled. Her perpetual sarcasm disappeared. She was like a totally new and different person—a cowering and obedient version of her former self. She came to believe that she *was* guilty. She had forsaken God and now she realized it. She had been sick all those years. And now she was well.

It was mid-1949 and the world was about to enter a new decade and a different era. The United States would soon be bogged down in a war in Korea. The people of Seattle feared an air raid on their mammoth Boeing plant south of town and were frantically building bomb shelters. The movie industry was dying in competition with television and the fate of a prewar movie star was hardly worth a mention on page ten, even in her hometown. But inside Steilacoom, there was great excitement about the recovery of Frances Farmer. She was soon integrated into the general population and the difference in her personality was startling. She was

224

meek and submissive and she generally did exactly as she was told. When she was forced into modeling hats at a fashion show given by one of the doctor's wives, she did not utter a single word of protest.

Later that year, Dr. Keller's office informed the Farmers of their daughter's remarkable and sudden recovery. Lillian Farmer had suffered a paralytic stroke some months before and now desperately needed someone to take care of her. In February, 1950, she wrote the doctors and they all agreed that Frances was ready to be released into her mother's custody. The last entry of her medical record states:

> Patient presented to staff. Nurse reports that on ward she is helpful to the feeble patients. Physically the patient is not strong.
>
> Staff unanimously recommends that parole be granted.

On the cold and rainy morning of March 23, 1950, Frances Farmer was led out of her ward, handed a change of street clothes, and taken to the front gate of Steilacoom to face the world. She took the bus back to Seattle and, with nothing more than a few unenthusiastic words of greeting, moved back into the family home on 47th Street. She had not seen a newspaper or heard a radio or held a conversation with an outsider for over five years. She had virtually no memory of any of the things that had happened to her. She was thirty-six years old.

Throughout the following months, Frances lived as a kind of maid around the family house—

taking care of her mother and cleaning up after her father (the two of them curiously reunited in their old age)—always with the threat hanging over her that she could be returned to Steilacoom without a moment's notice. The only time she ventured out of the house was to attend the early services at St. John the Baptist Episcopal Church on Sunday mornings. Sometimes old friends stopped by to see her, and they say they found a humorless and burned-out shell, a frightening counterfeit of what Frances had once been, endlessly speaking of herself as a "faceless sinner" who had finally found her way back to God.

47

As for the years of her life that followed, I desperately searched for some semblance of the old Frances—some spark of life, some hint of rebellion—but there was none. Throughout 1950, 1951, and 1952 she stayed in the family home taking care of her parents, a lonely and frightened figure of a human being. She did not read books or write poetry or pass the days with any kind of creative endeavor. When old friends dropped by to see her, she would run upstairs and lock herself in the bathroom. Neighborhood children would make up stories about her and hide outside the house to catch hurried glimpses of the neighborhood crazy lady. She was withdrawn and terrified of people and deathly afraid she would be returned to Steilacoom. She displayed, ironically, many of the very symptoms for which she was ostensibly sent to the institution in the first place.

She lived like this—in almost complete isolation—until the spring of 1953. It was not until May of that year—some two years after her release—that something at last began to stir within her. The neighbors recall that she suddenly seemed to become less frightened of people and more interested in the world. Slowly, she began to get out of the house and take walks around the neighborhood. In June, she started to ride the bus downtown and take long contemplative strolls in the city parks, as she had done years before. She showed such improvement that her brother, now a colonel in the Army, decided that it was time she helped out the failing family fortunes by getting a job.

Since she was still on parole from a mental institution, she would have to have her competency restored before she could legally seek employment in Washington State. The Farmers hired an attorney and petitioned the Superior Court to void her mother's guardianship and grant her competency. Nearly three years after release, she made a trip back to Steilacoom to be fully discharged. In the course of her final examination, she meekly told the doctors that her parents were old and ill and she had to support them. She said she would accept any kind of employment that would bring in a steady income. She said she had been very sick but, with the help of her treatments at Steilacoom, she had overcome her emotional problems. The doctors were impressed and on July 27, 1953, after over a decade of legal insanity, her competency and full civil rights were restored. The day the order went through, she went to the Olympic Hotel—the very place where the governor and all the dignitaries of the state had once gone to honor her—and got a job sorting dirty laundry.

The job seemed to bring her out of herself even more. She made a few friends among the maids and valets of the hotel and even began to go out on a few dates. Some of her escorts took her to cocktail lounges and to their apartments and they discovered—to their amazement—that Frances would not resist any advances they might make to her. By the beginning of 1954, she was going out to taverns and cocktail lounges almost every night of the week after work and making herself available to anyone who wanted to pick her up. I spoke to many people who remember her in this period and they all recall a quiet, still beautiful, rather strange woman with a cold, distant look in her eyes who drank heavily and was always good for a quick sexual encounter.

One of the men Frances dated was a city engineer named Alfred Lobley, a sensitive but rather hard-drinking man (the result, his relatives say, of a "bad war experience") whom she had met in a downtown cocktail lounge. He appears to have both felt genuinely sorry for Frances—he remembered the newspaper headlines and he had heard all the stories about her—and to have been fascinated with the idea of knowing a former movie queen. He took her out several times. He patiently tolerated her erratic behavior and patronized her strange phobias. He also got to know the elder Farmers, who liked him, and he spent many evenings sitting in front of the big stone fireplace chatting with them. He soon convinced them that the best possible thing for Frances would be to marry him. He was a responsible person and Frances obviously needed someone to take care of her, both emotionally and financially. The Farmers gladly gave their permission and the couple was married by a city clerk on April 17, 1954.

The marriage was, of course, doomed from

the start. Frances was still in a very eerie and disturbingly remote condition. A therapist who did research on the aftereffects of the Freeman transorbital experiments has said that many of the patients ceased their unmanageable behavior and functioned "normally" but became "zombielike creatures with poor ethical judgment." This is a fair description of Frances in 1954—a condition which Lobley did not understand and with which he could not even begin to deal. He died not many years later and never gave his side of the story, but after the novelty of the marriage wore off, his patience reportedly turned to fear and revulsion and he took to slapping her around the house and threatened to send her back to Steilacoom.

Then, after six months of this marriage, an extraordinary thing happened. One morning Frances got up, gathered together about seventy-five dollars, and, like the Frances Farmer of the '30s, impulsively stepped on the first bus going out of the city.

48

Frances utterly vanished for nearly three and a half years. No one in Seattle had any idea where she was living—or if she was living. In retrospect, it seems to have been a very wise decision on her part because there is evidence that all during those years people were intensely searching for her: her family, psychiatrists who wanted to show her off, politicians who, in those dark days of McCarthyism, wanted her to testify about her destructive flirtation with Communism. It was her most successful escape attempt and it seemed to offer some faint glimmer of hope that perhaps, just perhaps, she had not been completely broken in Steilacoom after all.

She apparently left Seattle intending to make an entirely new life for herself. She got off the bus in Eureka, California, choosing this small coastal city, apparently, for no other reason than the fact that she was out of money. She got a room in an old Victorian house and took a job as secretary in a photography studio under her first married name. Except for her employer in the studio, a kind and understanding man named Oscar Swanlund, no one in Eureka knew her true identity. She wanted, she

231

told him, to fit in and lose herself in a small-town existence.

Eureka is still a small, rather isolated city in the redwood region of northern California and an almost perfect place to hide from the world. I spent several hours wandering around talking to the townspeople and many of them remembered Frances Anderson. They remembered how she very mysteriously came to town and how she would freeze up when asked about her past. They also remembered how she went out of her way to be sociable and mix with the townspeople. She took instruction in the Roman Catholic faith, attended Mass regularly, and became somewhat active in church functions. She seemed to try very hard in those first few months to become part of the fabric of this town.

But try as she did, she was never really able to make that adjustment. She was totally unable to relate to other people, and in the light of everything that had happened to her, it is not difficult to understand why. Patients who have received a single series of electroshock treatments have often suffered so much brain damage that they are never quite the same again. Frances had received steady, intensive shock over a period of six years. Patients who have received a single dose of a single psychedelic drug have been known to suffer a lifetime of religious visions and paranoid reactions. Frances had been subjected to practically every experimental drug that was known to medical science. Moreover, the best part of her—her imagination—had almost certainly been surgically tampered with, and although she had no memory of it—or memory of much of anything that had happened to her in the last ten years—she must have known that some essential part of her was missing.

There were times when the past intruded on her new life and almost gave her away. The un-American witch-hunt and blacklist were now in full force, and she could not pick up a newspaper without reading about some former member of the Group Theater shamelessly kowtowing to the Mc-Carthyites—including Clifford Odets and Elia Kazan, both of whom became "friendly" witnesses. The story is told in Eureka that Frances one day picked up a copy of the conservative magazine *American Mercury* and read an article by Leif Erickson denouncing his political past that sent her into weeks of paranoia:

> For a period of years I . . . disgraced my profession and did a certain amount of damage to this country by giving the Communist front organizations aid and comfort. I won't use the alibi that "so did hundreds of other people in show business." I'm concerned with what Erickson did.
>
> I've read testimony and statements given by my fellow actors who whimper that they "didn't know the gun was loaded"; however, when I gave money and the use of my name to the Abraham Lincoln Brigade, I blinked at the fact that the boys who approached me backstage in *Golden Boy* in 1937 were doing a job for the Communists. When I went to a

233

"Rally for China" in the same year, I had a hunch that the comrades were pulling the strings. I gave my name to a couple of other fronts and no one had to twist my arm. . . .

I'm no mental giant, but I know the only way I can clear that past record of mine is to get out and prove I'm anti-Communist. Sulking, denying, or dodging the question isn't the solution. There's only one test that the public can apply to a guy like myself—what's he doing against Communism.

It is a good question. If you really want to, it isn't hard for an actor to find ways to fight Communism. There's the Motion Picture Alliance in Hollywood, a really tough bunch of Red-beaters who've been smeared and condemned by the comrades and the pinkos and the punkos for years, but who have gone on punching the dickens out of the conspiracy. I joined. So can you. . . .

Let's forget the Communist-inspired squeals about "blacklisting." No loyal producer or director has any business hiring an actor who for ten years fronted for subversion and still refuses to tell the truth or to fight the Reds. If this type of actor doesn't know the score by now, let him starve to death and please omit the flowers. . . .

Before long, Frances had taken to picking up a bottle after work and staying in her room each night and drinking it alone. She worked very hard during the day (and became "the most devoted assistant Mr. Swanlund ever had") but she was otherwise a virtual recluse, drinking herself into a stupor night after night. Weeks and months and even years passed without the slightest incident or change in her life. She became known to the people of Eureka as an odd, very quiet and unemotional, very remote woman with a perpetual smell of liquor on her breath, and all those years later they would find it almost impossible to believe that she had once been a major motion-picture star.

During this period, both her parents died. Lillian had grown progressively irrational over the years and her son's family had even tried to have *her* committed to Steilacoom. (She had dramatically fled to her lawyer, Lady Willie Forbus, who successfully prevented the move.) She later went to California to live with her daughter Rita and one day in March, 1955, she suddenly died of a stroke. Her husband, who had already been placed in a rest home paid for by the Elks Club, lived on for another year—no more weak and ineffectual in old age than he had been during the rest of his life—and finally died peacefully in his sleep at the age of eighty-five.

Frances was tracked down by the local Social Security office and told the news. She had been named her mother's sole heir and consequently was granted ownership of the family home in Seattle. She didn't seem to react to her parents' death very much one way or the other. She stayed in Eureka and continued her life of quiet routine, disturbed only by the fact that her anonymity had been partially destroyed. Throughout 1956 and early 1957,

235

she lived a quiet, semialcoholic existence with no connection to Seattle or the rest of her family. She might very well have lived this way for the rest of her life had not a small-time entrepreneur named Lee Mikesell recognized her buying liquor one night in 1957.

Mikesell was a pudgy man in his late forties who called himself a "show business consultant." Finding Frances Farmer on the street of Eureka, California, was the most incredible stroke of luck in a career almost totally devoid of luck. He recognized her at once, pursued her, took her to dinner, and tried to convince her to face her past and make a comeback. He told her that she was an actress ("it's in your every move and gesture") and that she could never be happy or fulfilled with life in any other capacity. He told her that he would become her manager and guide her back to her rightful place in the American theater. She numbly listened to him and part of her believed everything he said.

Mikesell officially ended her exile in the first week of April, 1957. He contacted neighbors in Seattle to find out the status of her property. He engaged an attorney and obtained her a divorce from Alfred Lobley. He put her on a diet, rushed her through a complete beauty treatment, and kept her away from liquor. Then he moved her to San Francisco, got her a job at the reception desk of the Sheraton-Palace Hotel, and started a major press campaign to promote the comeback of Frances Farmer.

49

Nineteen fifty-seven was something of a banner year for true-confession stories about the tragic lives of former movie stars. Films and books like *I'll Cry Tomorrow* (Lillian Roth) and *Too Much, Too Soon* (Diana Barrymore) were doing so well and were so prevalent that they were beginning to constitute a genre in American popular culture, the formula being that of a famous unloved woman moving from tragedy to tragedy and from bottle to bottle until she hits bottom and is finally rescued through the love of a good man. When the word got out in show business circles that Frances Farmer was on the comeback trail after just such a life experience and was willing to make a true confession about it, the offers began to pour in.

This immediate response was amplified by the fact that in the late '50s, mental illness was suddenly a subject that everyone seemed willing to talk about, and producers and agents and columnists were stepping all over each other trying to be "understanding." Ed Sullivan gave Frances her first big break on his television show in June. After a long and patronizing speech about how this pathetic woman had triumphed over nearly two decades of

237

mental illness, he let her sing two folk songs to the accompaniment of an acoustic guitar. After this boost, she embarked on a monumental struggle to train her memory to retain lines. Two months later, she appeared on stage in Bucks County, Pennsylvania, in *The Chalk Garden*. International News Service reported:

> After fifteen years of obscurity in which she won back her health and peace of mind, Frances Farmer returned to the theater tonight.
>
> And the former movie star who suffered a tragic breakdown in 1942 says "It's just like being home."
>
> Miss Farmer, now a mature forty, but still slim and attractive, played the lead in *The Chalk Garden* at Bucks County Playhouse in the appropriately named town of New Hope. She was a fresh-faced beauty of twenty-five when she last acted.
>
> She says her role is the first step on the road back to Broadway—and possibly Hollywood.
>
> In the play ironically she portrays a woman who is trying to pick up the threads of her life after being away from society for fifteen years.
>
> One of her lines is:
>
> "I value my fifteen years—they made me."
>
> Backstage Miss Farmer paraphrased that

line. "I haven't lost a thing. I feel as if I've gained a great deal."

The blond stately actress said she was "not a bit nervous" despite her long absence from the theater.

She stayed at the playhouse for short runs in *The Magic and the Loss* and *The Jamison Affair,* and then in December she appeared in a *Playhouse 90* production called "Reunion" with Hugh O'Brian and Martha Hyer. It took her many weeks to learn her part, a delay that infuriated the rest of the cast, but, remarkably under the circumstances, her performance was credible and received polite notices.

The highlight of her comeback campaign came on January 27, 1958, when Frances stepped on stage at an NBC television studio as Ralph Edwards ripped the ribbon off the book of "This Is Your Life—Frances Farmer." Belle McKenzie, Glenn Hughes, and several others from the University of Washington drama department who had figured prominently in her life flew down from Seattle. It was the only time in the long run of the show that a featured celebrity was warned in advance of her surprise. When Mikesell was making the arrangements, Edwards was reportedly so concerned that Frances might have a breakdown on national television that he refused to go ahead without this precaution.

I managed to get a video tape of that program, and seeing it was a devastating experience. The last time I had seen Frances on film was in *Son of Fury,* in which she had never looked more stunning. In front of the television cameras all those years later, she looked almost catatonic. Edwards skipped over her life rather hurriedly (he asked her point-blank if she was an alcoholic or a drug addict) and concentrated on her amazing rehabilitation ("A great Hollywood star returns from the depths of mental illness," he said with oozing admiration to a blank stare). He said he had telephoned some 125 producers and asked them to watch the show for consideration of Frances for leading roles in future films. To the embarrassment of everyone present, Frances barely uttered a word during the entire half hour. It was, one of the participants would remember, "a maudlin, humiliating experience, a complete fiasco, and quite possibly the most embarrassing *This Is Your Life* in the history of that embarrassing series."

Despite this catastrophe, the offers continued to come in during the first part of 1958. She appeared in a *Studio One* production with Margaret O'Brien (taking a few days out of the filming to get married to Mikesell in Las Vegas) and an episode of *Treasury Agent* with Lloyd Nolan. She did several weeks of stock in Traverse City, Michigan, and back again in Pennsylvania. She even returned to the Paramount lot and played a small part in a grade-B teen-age exploitation picture called *The Party Crashers*, starring Connie Stevens and Bobby Driscoll. She tried very hard, but ultimately it seemed to be no use. She could not adequately memorize lines. She did not respond to the proper cues. She often appeared on the set drunk. All the old drive, the mystical beauty, the exciting sense of timing, were gone. Whatever the magic was that had made her a great star was completely burned out, and there was not even enough left to make a credible character actress.

When the interest in her comeback began to wane, she went into an even sadder and more humiliating true-confession period ("The Shocking True Story of Frances Farmer as Told to..."). Mikesell set up a series of interviews and she confessed at great length about her sins before God entered her life in the mental institution—her atheism, her flirtation with Communism, and so on. (Most of it was made up—the various treatments had played havoc with her memory and she found it virtually impossible to recall even major incidents in her life accurately.) In February, she confessed to Gerold Frank in the pages of *Coronet* ("The Return of an Actress"). In May, she confessed to Edward Keyes in a long three-part series that appeared in *American Weekly,* the Hearst newspapers' magazine supplement ("I Climb Out of the Depths"). She related how she had been an irritable and unlikable movie star and how she had gone crazy and been saved through the miracles of psychiatry and religion. She closed the Hearst piece by saying: "That night I knelt and thanked Him, who led me out of the exile of despair and gave me another chance. I shall always thank Him.... I am very much in love and think that, from now on, life is going to be wonderful."

241

50

But life did not turn out to be wonderful at all. She was, in fact, never quite able to bring off any kind of permanent comeback. She was never able to get along with other people without feeling suspicious of their motives. She was subject to great lapses of memory and fits of paranoia. The marriage to Mikesell broke up when he couldn't get her any more jobs, and within a year he was suing her for the impossible sum of a quarter of a million dollars. Her drinking problem got steadily worse until she acquired the reputation of being a chronic alcoholic. By the end of the summer of 1958, she could no longer even get regional theater engagements and after a not terribly successful six-day run of *Chalk Garden* at the Avondale Playhouse in Indianapolis, she found herself destitute and stranded.

Indianapolis is a flat, politically conservative, somewhat provincial city in the very heart of Middle America. It is a city without any kind of identifying focus, a city that has always suffered something of an inferiority complex in regard to cultural matters, constantly looking jealously over its shoulder at Chicago or Philadelphia or even St. Louis. In such a city there was always a place for someone who had once been the toast of New York and Hollywood. When word of her financial plight got around, she was promptly offered a job hosting the afternoon movie on a local television station. With a little makeup and proper lighting she could still look striking and she was able to exude a certain detached charm on the air which, I suppose, made the whole idea seem feasible. Having nowhere else to go and nothing better to do, she accepted the offer. The program was called *Frances Farmer Presents,* and on it she introduced grade-B movies, did commercials, and, when she felt up to it, chatted with visiting celebrities.

When I got to Indianapolis, it was late fall and the city was bathed in fallen leaves and autumn browns. I immediately found many, many people who remembered Frances from the years when she did the show and they all half-smiled at the mention of her name. She seems to have become known as a quiet and harmless drunk, a fixture around town whose eccentric behavior was tolerated by Indianapolis society with wry amusement. She made several close friends—particularly a young widow who would figure prominently in the rest of her life named Jeanira Ratcliffe—and bought a modest house, which everyone said she grew to love. She generally fell in with the routine of the station and her co-workers say she functioned as a kind of robot—every single word she uttered on the air had to be written down for her.

The video tapes that survive of the period show a reasonably intelligent but distant and somewhat absentminded woman who seems never quite in control of the situation. ("Hello, ladies and gentlemen," she would invariably say. "This is (long pause) Frances Farmer. Today's movie is *Lone Gun,* an exciting (long pause) Western, loaded with (long pause) action and thrills.") It was a depressing spectacle to see someone who had once been such an artist trying so hard to drum up enthusiasm for trashy movies with which she formerly would not have even considered associating herself, putting up with the whims of semi-celebrities without a tenth of her former talent, and humoring right-wing political figures whose very presence once would have deeply offended her.

There was not much to learn about those years in Indianapolis. At one point she was named Indiana's "Business Woman of the Year," though no one could understand exactly why, and she appeared in two student productions at nearby Purdue University without a great deal of success. She numbly judged fashion shows, attended openings of supermarkets, and otherwise played the part of a minor celebrity of the city. She did not read very much or take delight in the theater or enjoy the company of people. She did not take an active interest in politics or community affairs or join in the civil rights struggle. She never spoke of her earlier life without wildly exaggerating her guilt and fantasizing great sexual excesses. She stayed in her home and apparently became more and more dependent on her friend, Jean Ratcliffe, who looked after her affairs and provided her with desperately needed emotional support.

By the early part of 1964, the ratings of the

show had drastically fallen off. Her drinking had made her look bad physically and had given her an increasingly nasty disposition. The years in Steilacoom had taken their toll and she was in terrible shape by this time, with nagging low blood pressure, ulcers, and a persistent rash spreading over her entire body. She was beginning to let her appearance run down and soon became an embarrassment to the station. Her co-workers of the time describe her as a woman "totally unable to cope with things right in front of her—much less cope with tomorrow."

In the early spring of 1964, the NBC *Today Show* decided to do an hour-long profile on her "amazing recovery" from a lifetime of mental illness. A camera crew was sent to Indianapolis to film her in her home environment, and then she was flown to New York to appear on the show with host John Daly. The network had submitted the questions to be asked her to the station in advance, but somehow Frances never got a chance to see them. When Daly asked her about her drinking and mental breakdowns, she was thrown totally off guard and couldn't cope with the rest of the interview. She mumbled something about not wanting to talk about it and then denounced her parents. After this humiliating incident, she became too emotionally distraught to work. She stayed drunk for weeks on end, and the station finally decided she was clearly more trouble than she was worth. After several incidents later that year in which she appeared intoxicated before the cameras, she was summarily fired.

245

51

I stayed on in Indianapolis for several more days. There was a long line of people there who knew Frances in those years, but they all seemed to know a different Frances, as if the real person had died in the treatment rooms of Steilacoom and an imposter had taken her place. As I spoke to these people, I found myself looking for, hoping for, some faint sign that the old Frances would somehow reemerge and reassert herself in the end.

But without a job or even the prospect of a job, she withdrew into herself even further and her drinking escalated. Years went by and nothing really changed in her life at all. The conflict in Viet Nam grew month by month and year by year into a national horror story. Long-haired students took over their universities. Leaders were assassinated. Inner cities burned. The look and feel of the country changed, but Frances—one of the most rebellious voices of her generation—remained in the house on a middle-class street in Indianapolis with the curtains closed.

There were times in those years when she tried very hard to get back into some creative work—without much success. Undoubtedly, the effects of her various treatments wore off somewhat as the years passed, but her creative impulse never really recovered from the years of massive psychiatric assault. She published one short poem in a local literary anthology, which showed some flashes of the old fire, but nothing came of it and she never really tried to write poetry again. She was very effective as the embittered millionairess in a student production of *The Visit* at Purdue University, and gave some effective dramatic readings at the Indianapolis Art Museum for a time, but after a while even these efforts became difficult for her and she gave them up.

By 1966, Frances had become almost totally dependent on her relationship with Jean Ratcliffe. Ratcliffe was a rather hard, mysterious woman, a reclusive figure who was something of an enigma even to her closest friends. Frances had lived with her off and on in the past and, though she vehemently denied it to the very end, they were widely regarded around town as a Lesbian couple. After Frances was fired from her job, Ratcliffe seemed effectively to take over her life. In the later '60s, people say that Frances simply did not and could not function without the support and approval of Jean Ratcliffe.

During the years Frances had worked in television, she had earned a good salary, in excess in $18,000 a year, most of which she had carefully saved. In 1968, she and Ratcliffe decided to use this money to form a corporation to manufacture cosmetics. It is not clear exactly how it happened, but after a year of struggle, the business went broke and Frances lost every penny she had saved. The house which had given her so much security and which she had grown to love so much was heavily mortgaged and had to be sold. At the end of 1969 the two women moved to an old abandoned farmhouse just outside the Indianapolis city limits to live a pastoral and secluded life with a houseful of dogs and cats.

Earlier that year, Frances had approached a writer named Lois Kibbee about doing a book on her life. Frances had heard good reports of Kibbee's biography of Christine Jorgensen and she eventually invited the writer to Indianapolis to talk about the project. Kibbee came to town—rather shocked to be met at the airport by a very intoxicated, gray-haired old lady—and gradually became quite fond of Frances. They decided that their book would be a story of survival—of the internal means by which Frances was able to survive such a life ordeal. Over a period of about a year, they taped a number of conversations, but the project got stymied when Kibbee had to stop and do editorial work on another book.

In April, 1970, Frances suddenly had great difficulty swallowing. Two days later she became seriously ill. After several weeks of intense throat pain, she went to a doctor and her condition was diagnosed as cancer of the esophagus. She was given X-ray treatments, which were ineffective, and the condition became worse. She had no money to pay the doctors so she was taken as a charity case to an Indianapolis hospital for more treatments. These also proved ineffective, and soon all hope of recovery was given up. She remained in the hospital, moving in and out of consciousness until she died a slow and painful death on the first day of August, 1970.

The funeral was held on a bright, sultry day in a cemetery just outside Indianapolis. Six women friends acted as pallbearers. Nationally, her death went almost unnoticed. In Seattle, the city that had persecuted her all her life, her obituary was buried in the back pages. It read simply:

> Seattle-born film actress Frances Farmer, a onetime downtown theater usherette who went on to a career mixed with success and personal tragedy in Hollywood, died of cancer Saturday in Indianapolis. She was fifty-six.
>
> Miss Farmer's personal and professional life read like a weekday soap opera.
>
> She came from a broken home; after beginning to make it in the movies the pressure got too great and she started drinking, was married several times and confined to mental institutions twice for treatment of schizophrenia, and finally settled down in 1958 when she moved to Indianapolis. . . .
>
> She had no children and there are no immediate survivors.

Immediately after Frances' death, Lois Kibbee withdrew from the book project and Jean Ratcliffe picked it up. Over the next year or so, she fashioned much of the material Frances had given her into a first-person "autobiography." She seems

249

to have invented a number of sensational scenes, glorified the character of Jean Ratcliffe excessively in the last few chapters, and finally—as a curious closing touch—dedicated the book to herself.

52

I flew back to Seattle one day toward the end of October, 1976. That night *Come and Get It* was on a Canadian television station and I stayed up to catch some of it. It had been well over three years since I first stumbled onto this movie and it still had a powerful effect on me. I ended up watching most of it over again, in fact. The images of the twenty-one-year-old Frances were so beautiful and full of life—so charged with youth and positive energy—that there was something uplifting in seeing them again after everything I had learned.

The next morning I drove to my office and went through the accumulated back mail. In one large manila envelope, there was a copy of something called the *National Tattler,* containing an interview with Edith Farmer Elliot in which she told how the Communists had driven her sister crazy ("Sister of Late Movie Queen Frances Farmer Claims Communists 'Used' the Star to Boost Their Cause and Drove Her Insane"). There was a letter from a psychiatrist in Portland who said the real tragedy of the Frances Farmer affair was that anyone would question the wonderful and dedicated men of Steilacoom and the marvelous work they had

251

done there. And there was an affectionate, anecdotal letter from a woman who remembered Frances as a little blond girl romping around the neighborhood on SW 47th Street.

There was also a report by one of my co-workers on the fate of some of the characters involved with the case. It indicated that Dr. Nicholson had died in 1948, one of the most revered men in the state's medical history. His friend Judge Frater was struck down by a heart attack a few years later, and was widely mourned as a great patriot and pioneering legal figure. Dr. Hockett, head of Harborview Hospital in the early '40s, later came forward with shocking charges that he had been subjected to undue political pressure in his administration, but he was quickly fired and his charges were ignored. Dr. Walter Freeman went on to world fame and television talk-show appearances and died in the late '60s, his reputation only slightly tarnished by the parade of victims he left behind. Many of the doctors who had treated Frances were still alive and were among the most respected leaders of the psychiatric establishment of the Northwest.

While I was reading the report, my editor—a new one, since Ruth Howell had died in the intervening years—called me in and wanted to know if I had at last solved the mystery of Frances Farmer. And I had to tell him that I didn't know. I didn't know if the complete truth would ever be known. I didn't know if she had been insane, because after all this time I still had no idea what insanity was—and I doubt if anyone who treated her did. She was definitely troubled and difficult. She suffered from an eccentricity that may or may not have been hereditary and a paranoia that turned out to be quite justified. But she was never really violent—except in self-defense—or suicidal or any kind of public danger, and most of the evidence indicates that her more erratic actions were the result rather than the cause of her treatments.

The only thing that seemed certain was that there was an extraordinary streak of rebellion in this woman's personality that drove her to accomplish great things and manifested itself in many strange and unique ways—a lack of material concern, a biting, sarcastic wit, a blunt honesty, a hatred of injustice, a fierce competition with her mother and her family values, perhaps even a latent homosexuality that never quite made it to the surface. And these qualities irritated people, pushed them, made them feel uncomfortable, and because she made them feel uncomfortable, they saw in her actions exactly what they wanted to see and were quite willing to accept any meaningless pseudoscientific labels that might be placed on her by figures in authority.

I could not say, for sure, whether or not the long-rumored tight political conspiracy to put Frances Farmer away ever took place. Certainly there was a tight cover-up—on every level for over thirty years—but this might be true of any embarrassing psychiatric case. I told him that the theory of a Communist conspiracy seemed no more than a far-fetched effort by Lillian Farmer to absolve herself of guilt. The right-wing vigilante conspiracy, of course, was a bit more plausible. Given the times, the place, the personal testimony, and the personalities in-

253

volved, it even seems likely. But probably the most compelling argument against it was that it was totally unnecessary. The commitment laws were so structured that no one had to sit in a dark room and conspire. No one involved—not Frater or Nicholson or Lillian Farmer, not the American Vigilantes of Washington or the doctors of Steilacoom, not even Walter Freeman—had to do anything that was flagrantly illegal. This was the most chilling aspect of the entire case.

It seemed to me that the real conspiracy against Frances Farmer was the conspiracy of psychiatry against any individual who happens to be different. I told him that if there was any single truth to the story of Frances Farmer, it was that she found herself the prime attraction of a psychiatric sideshow that allowed no possible escape and led to one inevitable conclusion. Because she was one of the most glamorous and complicated women of her generation, she became a prize guinea pig for arrogant and ruthless men who were determined to remold her into a more acceptable version of herself. When they could not save her by their standards, they destroyed her. She was quite simply—and in the very truest sense of the word—a martyr. And somehow that fact would not seem half so clear or believable in her life as it would be in the long and disturbing shadow of her death.

254

Epilogue

The first thing an investigative reporter learns about the mental health industry is that it does not like to talk about its old psychiatric cases—*any* old psychiatric cases. This reticence is less a frightened cover-up than a painful memory: the victims of 40 years of radical shock treatments and some 50,000 lobotomies in state mental hospitals do not make for good public relations. When I tried to confront various psychiatric authorities with the story of Frances Farmer, for the most part they simply refused to discuss it. Many of them looked sympathetic and shrugged it off as a "terrible" thing that happened a long, long time ago. They all insisted that such a thing could never happen today.

But the sad and appalling truth is that the Frances Farmer case is not merely an isolated incident dredged up from another era. It is extraordinary only in terms of the woman's fame and great visibility (and, indeed, there are many other examples of the negative effects of radical treatment on such celebrities as Ernest Hemingway, Judy Garland, and Vivien Leigh). The literature of psychiatric abuse chronicles thousands of more recent and equally disturbing cases—hyperactive nine-

255

year-olds lobotomized in Mississippi, homosexuals shocked into insensibility in England, Steilacoom-like conditions in Massachusetts and Indiana and Virginia. While I was doing research in the Midwest, a Hungarian immigrant was arrested there and subjected to extensive shock therapy because he didn't speak English and his dialect had been diagnosed by a psychiatrist as the babblings of psychosis. In California, eight Stanford University researchers who had themselves admitted to a dozen different mental hospitals by pretending to be insane found they could not overcome the label "schizophrenic" no matter how normal they subsequently behaved. (They were finally released after outside intervention by the project director.) Similar stories abound.

The fact is that surprisingly little has changed in the 35 years since Frances Farmer first came under the thumb of organized psychiatry. Many states—including Washington—have passed new laws which make involuntary commitment more difficult, but the potential for abuse remains enormous in a field where a mental patient's future may be decided on the most arbitrary and subjective grounds. Psychiatry often seems like a science built on sand, with a set of premises that shift like the tides. As a discipline, psychiatry has never been able to define precisely what is normal (or abnormal) behavior, and thus it inevitably ends up enforcing conformity to whatever the current community and government standards happen to be— whether defined by Fascist Italy, National Socialist Germany, Soviet Russia or the State of Washington.

In the past decade, the tide of public opinion has swung heavily against traditional psychiatry. Recent research indicates that schizophrenia is attributable to an excess of receptors in the brain for a chemical messenger called dopamine, a condition which is probably related to heredity and nutrition. And this could conceivably make much of the practice of psychiatry obsolete. Laing, Szasz, and other radical therapists are still gunning away at their colleagues, and virtually every theory and treatment has been challenged by one eminent psychiatrist or another. An increasing number of studies made by psychiatry itself, in fact, confirms the suspicion that mental patients often get well faster when given no treatment than when given conventional psychiatric therapy.

And yet, despite this landslide of damning evidence and new information, institutional psychiatry has still managed to hang on to its extra-legal power and medieval treatments. Psychiatric associations have battled off attempts to outlaw shock therapy in numerous states. The big pharmaceutical companies continue recklessly to market the maze of mind controlling drugs before their side effects are thoroughly known. The population of the 337 public mental institutions—including Western State Hospital at Steilacoom—has swelled to nearly four times the prison population, and in the past decade more Americans died in mental hospitals than died in battle in all wars except World War II.

Even more ominous is the fact that, after a 15-year fallow period in which psychosurgery fell from fashion, it is now undergoing a world-wide resurgence. Various subtle and almost undetectable operations with names like "hypothalamotomy" and "amygdalotomy"—operations which largely grew out of the Freeman transorbital experiments of the late '40s—have been developed and widely performed in the '70s. According to some estimates, nearly 1,000 lobotomies a year take place and as the procedures become more simple and refined, the possibility of their use by a totalitarian government as a means of mass mind control becomes chillingly plausible.

The mentality of the system which deals with supposedly abnormal behavior is virtually unchanged since the 1940s. The chance of an individual like Frances Farmer being trapped and destroyed by this system is as real today as it was then. The bitter legacy of her story is not that such a fate could strike a public figure protected by the privileges of celebrity, but that it can happen to anyone.

Acknowl-
edgment

This book came about through the efforts of a great many people not specifically mentioned in the text.

At the top of this list is Steven R. Heard, who, both as a member of the Citizens Commission on Human Rights and as a personal friend, worked continually over the past four years getting at some semblance of the truth in this case.

The original Frances Farmer article in the *Seattle Post-Intelligencer,* from which all the information contained in the book grew, would never have been published had not Mike Conant, Lettie Gavin, and Lou Guzzo bulldozed it through against considerable editorial opposition in 1974.

Also helpful on the staff of the *P-I* were publisher and movie addict Bob Thompson, editor Jack Doughty, book editor Archie Satterfield, and Florence Frye, surely the world's most resourceful newspaper librarian.

Other journalists in Seattle who in one way or another contributed to the book are Tim Menees, Mike Henderson, Sam A. Angeloff, Thom Gunn, and the late Jack Vanderman, who did pioneering in-

259

vestigative reporting in the field of mental health abuse and kindly shared it with me.

In New York, those especially helpful were Frederic Hills of McGraw-Hill, Burton Beals, agent Knox Burger, the late James Jones, who was a constant source of encouragement, and columnist Rex Reed, who singlehandedly kept the memory of Frances Farmer alive over the past several years.

In Los Angeles, Tim and Marie Yates, Heber Jentzsch, and Noel Marshall and his wife Tippi Hedren all gave unselfishly of their time and talents, and are largely responsible for getting the project off the ground.

And lastly, I want to recognize the contribution of the Birkland girls of West Seattle, who are growing up in the shadow of Frances Farmer and who, in a way they may never fully understand, inspired this book from beginning to end.